Increasing Professionalism in Public Finance Management

A WORLD BANK STUDY

Increasing Professionalism in Public Finance Management

A Case Study of the United Kingdom

Sarah Jane Squire and Ivor Beazley

WORLD BANK GROUP

Contents

Preface		*ix*
Acknowledgments		*xi*
Executive Summary		*xiii*
Abbreviations		*xv*
Chapter 1	**External Environment**	1
	Policies and Leadership	1
	Renewed Political Commitment and the Role and Status of the Finance Profession	5
	Success?	8
	Outlook for the Future	9
	Obstacles to Change	15
	Annex 1A: The National Audit Office: Helping the Nation Spend Wisely	16
	Annex 1B: Managing Public Money: Guidance to Civil Servants on How to Handle Public Funds	17
	Annex 1C: Finance Transformation Programme	18
	Annex 1D: Managing Taxpayers' Money Wisely: Commitment to Action 2011	19
	Annex 1E: The Civil Service Reform Plan	21
	Annex 1F: The Review of Financial Management 2013 and Progress on Recommendations	25
	Annex 1G: Forecasting	28
	Notes	29
Chapter 2	**Organizational Framework**	31
	Network, Responsibilities, Capacity, and Effectiveness	31
	Training Providers	35
	Annex 2A: Internal Audit Function	38
	Annex 2B: The Procurement Function	41
	Annex 2C: The Project Delivery Function	45
	Annex 2D: Chartered Finance and Accountancy Institutes	47
	Annex 2E: AAT: Association of Accounting Technicians	50

Annex 2F: CIIA: The Chartered Institute of Internal
   Auditors   51
Annex 2G: CIPS: The Chartered Institute of
   Purchasing and Supply   53
Annex 2H: Examples of Specialist Public Financial
   Management Areas   55
Annex 2I: Civil Service Talent Toolkit   57
Annex 2J: Civil Service Local: Cross-Government
   Mentoring   59
Annex 2K: Graduate Entry to the Civil Service
   Fast Stream   60
Notes   63

Chapter 3   Supporting Human Resource Management Processes   65
Structure of Jobs   65
Grading and Pay   66
Recruitment and Selection   66
Transfers   67
Annex 3A: HM Treasury Target Operating Model
   Taxonomy   67
Annex 3B: The Role of Finance Business Partner   69
Annex 3C: Trainee Accountancy Allowance and
   Progression Arrangements   70
Annex 3D: Civil Service Resourcing Vacancy Filling
   Scheme   71
Note   72

Chapter 4   Professional Development Processes   73
Career Planning and Management   73
Training and Development—Design and Delivery   77
Annex 4A: The Civil Service Capabilities Plan   79
Annex 4B: Continuing Professional Development   81
Notes   81

Chapter 5   Results and Indicators   83
Attraction and Retention   83
Skills and Competencies   84
Rewards   86
Annex 5A: Civil Service People Survey 2015   88
Notes   89

Appendix   Timeline: Developing Professional Finance in Government   91

References   **93**

Box

A1D.1   Professions of Senior Civil Service Posts as of
         April 2012   21

Figures

1.1   The Civil Service's Good Finance Model   9
1.2   Government Receipts and Expenditure, 2009–21   11
1.3   Number of Finance Function Staff, 2009–15   12
A1G.1   Finance and Analyst Collaboration on Forecasting   28
A2I.1   Use of the 9 Box Grid   58
A2K.1   Steps in the Civil Service Fast Stream Process   61
A3A.1   HM Treasury Finance Target Operating Model   68
A3C.1   Allowance Paid to Trainee   70
5.1   Finance Staff Working Outside Mainstream Finance, 2009–13 84
A5A.1   Civil Service People Survey 2015, Civil Service Benchmark
         Scores, November 2015   88

Tables

1.1   Percentage of Qualified Finance Staff, 2009–15   12
2.1   Number of Finance Graduates, 2013   36
5.1   Completion of Courses in Priority Capability Areas   86

Preface

For many years, the World Bank and other development agencies have financed training as an important component of projects designed to strengthen public financial management (PFM). However, despite these investments, relatively few developing countries have succeeded in creating an environment where PFM skills are systematically developed and maintained. Many countries still struggle to recruit, develop, and retain staff with the requisite professional skills in such areas as accounting and auditing. At the same time, the business of financial management in government is becoming more complex. Countries are moving from cash to accruals accounting, and from line item budgeting to performance budgeting. New ways of delivering services (for example, public private-partnerships and outsourcing) demand a new level of sophistication in public procurement and project management. Governments have also committed themselves to greater transparency and accountability and are making ever-greater use of information technology as a tool for managing public services and improving financial management.

With this in mind, the World Bank, with financial support from the Ministry of Finance of the Russian Federation, has initiated a study to look at and learn from the experiences of different countries in developing financial management skills. The study looks at a broad set of issues that all affect financial management skills. These include recruitment, job specification, training and professional development, career management, pay, and organizational and institutional arrangements.

A mix of countries was selected for study to capture not only some of the more interesting reform efforts, but also to reflect the fact that a variety of different approaches may result in success in countries that have different administrative traditions and cultures. In the United Kingdom, successive governments, having recognized that improving financial management skills is critical to making public services more efficient and effective, have taken positive actions to address weaknesses in this area. Other countries being studied in this series are France, the Kazakhstan, the Netherlands, the Russian Federation, the Republic of Korea, and South Africa.

Research Methodology

The research for this report focused on the central Civil Service bodies in England. No other work was conducted in Wales, Scotland, or Northern Ireland, all of which, being devolved, have the option not to follow certain guidance from the center in London.

The main approaches to the research were interviews (telephone or in person), a focus group of PFM specialists held at the Chartered Institute of Public Finance and Accountancy (CIPFA), and a review of documents on the Internet and from other sources. Information relating to the procurement, commercial, and project management professions and to oversight exercised by the Cabinet Office for these professions, was obtained primarily via the Internet; it was not possible to discuss the report with the Cabinet Office during the research.

The authors are particularly grateful for the support and material provided by members of the government finance function (previously the Government Finance Profession) and CIPFA. The researcher met, talked with by telephone, or e-mailed the following people:

AAT	Rob Alder, Business Development Manager
ACCA	Gillian Fawcett, Head of Public Sector
CIMA	Ben Lambert and Ian Stapleton, employer relationship/student recruitment managers
CIPFA	Giles Orr, Head of Global Business Development; Manj Kalar, CIPFA Technical Manager Central Government
DWP	Two finance managers
GIAA	Deputy Head
HM Treasury	*2014 Government Finance Profession*: Skills capability and professionalism policy adviser Head of GFP resourcing (from DWP on secondment to HM Treasury) *2016 Government Finance Function*: Head of strategy and engagement, Finance Capability and Commercial, Public Spending Group Strategy and program manager, Finance Capability and Commercial, Public Spending Group
ICAEW	Jonathan Jones, Policy and Strategy Director; and Hazel Garvey, Director of Business Development
IIA	David Lyscom, Policy Director; with additional input from Alisdair McIntosh
Kaplan	Charles Gubbins, Head of Faculty, Kaplan Hawksemere
NAO	Mark Babbington, Director; Michael Kell, Chief Economist; Neil Sayers, Director
Public Chairs Forum	Chris Banks CBE, Chair
Focus Group	GFP Head of Resourcing for Government Finance Profession (from DWP on secondment to HM Treasury) Skills capability and professionalism policy adviser, HM Treasury Manj Kalar, CIPFA Technical Manager Central Government (previously with the Department of Local Government and the Home Office) Alison Sweeting, independent consultant (previously finance director, London Borough Tower Hamlets, and CIPFA lecturer/trainer) Graham Marsden, independent consultant (experience: financial management reviews of U.K. central government departments, international PFM assignments with OECD; and previously partner in PWC)

Acknowledgments

The authors of this case study, Sarah Jane Squire, a consultant based in the United Kingdom, and Ivor Beazley, a public sector specialist at the World Bank, are grateful to Her Majesty's Treasury and the Government Internal Audit Agency for their assistance in conducting the study and providing feedback on the draft report.

Executive Summary

In the United Kingdom, public servants manage almost 40 percent of national spending. They run highly complex businesses that affect the lives of millions of citizens, and their spending and investment decisions often dwarf those made by private companies. However, compared to private companies whose stock is publicly traded—where skilled finance professionals are routinely employed to control costs, monitor efficiency, and satisfy demands for financial information from shareholders, financial markets, tax authorities, and regulators—the government has been slow to recognize the importance of financial management skills. However, since the 1980s, efforts to professionalize public financial management have been gathering momentum and are now an integral part of the government's plans to control costs and improve the management of public services. This report examines the United Kingdom's reform path and describes how the government recruits, trains, manages, and rewards finance professionals.

The history of the British Civil Service has been punctuated by periods of politically and managerially inspired change. Some common threads are evident in these changes: enhancing the leadership qualities of civil servants; giving higher priority to resource management, results, and accountability; and improving professional and technical skills. The sustained fiscal pressures of the last five years have again highlighted the need to embrace financial skills as part of the attempt to shift public sector culture toward emphasizing value for money and results. The government's aim is to put finance at the center of decision making, and to deliver sustainable public services at lower cost. Two years after introducing a financial management reform program, the U.K. Treasury considers that it now has a sound platform for driving value and building capability across the government finance function.

The skills profile of public finance managers is also changing. Transactional services, previously carried out by more junior officers, are increasingly being outsourced to shared service centers (an initiative that is still at a relatively early stage); finance officers are now expected to become more commercially aware in order to manage and monitor these outsourced services and other significant contractual relationships. Her Majesty's Treasury is also encouraging finance staff to work more closely with nonfinance colleagues to improve the quality of forecasting and longer-term planning.

The United Kingdom is thus getting closer to the goal of putting finance at the heart of government. Three permanent secretaries are now professionally qualified accountants, reinforcing the importance of finance as a path to the top jobs. All directors general of finance are qualified accountants, reinforcing the importance of finance on the management agenda of their departments. Supporting these senior managers, the government is building a community of public financial management professionals to work in a wide range of roles. It is supporting those who have the potential to go further and faster than their peers and to allow the very best talent to be deployed to organizational priorities. The government is trying to break down the traditional silo approach, in which some professional groups were considered more equal than others, and enable individuals to move into areas such as finance if they have, or are willing to gain, appropriate skills.

The U.K. Civil Service has no problem attracting high-caliber recruits; the combination of intellectually challenging and rewarding work and a benefits package that stands up against private sector norms has in general been sufficient to attract and retain talented individuals. However, in the past, the Civil Service was less successful in creating rewarding careers for finance and other technical professionals. Although the government has made finance more attractive, it still must build commercial skills and expertise, particularly in managing major projects and acquisitions. The downsizing and restructuring of departments necessary to meet continuing fiscal constraints is likely to be the biggest test.

Abbreviations

AAT	Association of Accounting Technicians
ACA	Association of Chartered Accountants
ACCA	Chartered Association of Certified Accountants
ALB	Arm's-Length Body
BHBi	Birmingham City University Business School
BSc	bachelor of science degree
CBE	Commander of the British Empire
CCAB	Consultative Committee of Accountancy Bodies
CCS	Crown Commercial Services
CFPAB	Counter Fraud Professional Accreditation Board
CIA	certified internal auditor
CIIA	Chartered Institute of Internal Auditors
CIMA	Chartered Institute of Management Accountants
CIPFA	Chartered Institute of Public Finance and Accountancy
CIPS	Chartered Institute of Purchasing and Supply
CPD	continuing professional development
CSR	Civil Service Resourcing
DGPS	Director General of Public Spending and Finance
DWP	Department for Work and Pensions
ESF	European Social Fund
FBP	finance business partner
FM	financial management
FMI	Financial Management Initiative
FTP	Finance Transformation Programme
GAS	Government Accountancy Service
GFP	Government Finance Profession
GIA	Government Internal Audit
GIAA	The Government Internal Audit Agency
HM	Her Majesty's

HR	human resources
ICAEW	Institute of Chartered Accountants in England and Wales
ICAS	Institute of Chartered Accountants of Scotland
IIA	Institute of Internal Audit
IPA	Infrastructure Projects Authority
IPSAS	International Public Sector Accounting Standards
IRM	Institute for Risk Management
IT	information technology
MBA	master of business administration degree
MI	Management Information
MOD	Ministry of Defence
MP	Member of Parliament
MPA	Major Projects Authority
MPLA	Major Projects Leadership Academy
NAO	National Audit Office
OBR	Office for Budget Responsibility
OJT	on-the-job training
ONS	Office for National Statistics
OSCAR	Online System for Central Accounting and Reporting
PAC	Public Accounts Committee
PFM	public financial management
PLP	Project Leadership Programme
PSCR	public sector current receipt
SCS	Senior Civil Service
TME	total managed expenditure
VfM	value for money
VFS	Vacancy Filling Scheme
UCAS	Universities and Colleges Admissions Service

CHAPTER 1

External Environment

Policies and Leadership

It took political will, the determination of an "evangelical accountant" and persistent diplomacy to move Whitehall's finance professionals from the bean-counting hinter-lands to a central position where they could begin to ensure that the machinery of government was not only well-oiled, but cost-effective. (Civil Service 2012d)

In 1968, the Fulton Report (House of Commons 1968) called for more professional management at all levels in the Civil Service, including economic and business management. Focusing on the accountancy profession, the report noted that "Present practice in the Civil Service severely restricts the role of the accountant class and excludes its members from responsibility for financial control." However, it took another 14 years for the Government Accountancy Service (GAS), the forerunner of the current government finance function, to emerge from the prevailing "gifted amateur" generalist culture in the Civil Service.

A more important role for accountants was presaged by the formation of the GAS in 1982—although, perhaps illustrating the distance still to be travelled, the GAS was housed in the Department for Trade and Industry. This happened to be where the majority of accountants in government were located, but it was far from HM Treasury and the heart of public financial management (PFM). At that time, some departments "were still reluctant to see the significance of accounting information" (Civil Service 2012d) and the formation of GAS was intended to demonstrate the worth of PFM professionals in decision-making. The GAS aimed to increase the number of professional accountants across government, release them from their role of providing only technical advice, and offer them a career path to the most senior posts. Central to the success of GAS was ensuring that accountants built a network of influence with their peers, meeting together to share expertise and good practice.

The choice of the Department for Trade as the home for GAS was perhaps not so odd, given that business was the source of modern financial management practices. Those practices had an important part in the success of the Financial

Management Initiative (FMI), introduced with the GAS to identify an approach to measuring departmental performance against objectives. The GAS moved to the Treasury in 1984.

Introduction of the FMI

The FMI arrived in 1982. Backed by Prime Minister Thatcher and senior government figures, it aimed to promote in each department and organization a system in which managers at all levels have:

- A clear view of the objectives, and means to assess and, wherever possible, measure outputs or performance in relation to those objectives;
- Well-defined responsibility for making the best use of their resources, including a critical scrutiny of output and value for money (VfM); and
- The information (particularly about costs), the training, and the access to expert advice that they need to exercise their responsibilities effectively (House of Lords 1998).

The FMI involved relatively junior civil servants accepting responsibility for their own budgets. It envisaged the introduction into government financial management of "devolved budgeting" and "resource accounting," both of which required accountants to help managers enter the numbers. With some persuasion from the head of GAS, managers realized they needed more accountancy support.

The FMI should have reinforced the role of the GAS: for the first time accountants were seen as a mainstay of a major government initiative. However, the vast majority of civil servants still seemed reluctant to embrace the use of accountants. They were more concerned with obtaining a sufficient budget, maintaining harmony with their supervisors, and at all costs avoiding a qualification to their accounts and an appearance before the Public Accounts Committee[1] (PAC). It was a long time before the concept of VfM was really taken on board, and there are still pockets of resistance. The policy was to keep accountants at arm's length; they were seen as "a threat because they had the ability to challenge."[2]

Progress in PFM depended on the talent available, which in some departments was thin on the ground. A GAS Management Unit was created in the mid-1980s to act as a focus for the training and development of the accountancy profession within the government. After the training program was introduced, the number of accountants increased significantly, though they were not always put to best use. The Ministry of Defence (MOD), for example, introduced an academy to train a large number of accountants (Chartered Institute of Management Accountants, CIMA), but left many of them in "bean-counter" roles rather than using their talents to help the Ministry understand its costs.

Change for accountants did not come quickly; many left the Civil Service in the late 1980s as they realized that their careers would not take off. The private sector, which was at the time actively recruiting accountants and finance managers from all sectors, seemed more attractive and paid better.

Permanent secretaries and senior managers remained reluctant to allow finance-trained colleagues to have significant influence in decision-making. To counter this, and to strengthen leadership in finance, in 1986 "Heads of Accountancy Profession"[3] were introduced in each department. The accountancy heads, normally the most senior finance official, were charged with supporting more junior finance colleagues; departmental heads of profession reported to the then-head of GAS, who functioned as overall head of profession. The GAS encouraged the development of a network of accountancy heads to provide a voice for the profession at the departmental level and a forum for mutual support and sharing of good practice.

Increasing Importance of Finance
Where heads of profession proved effective—were seen as technically competent, persuasive, and committed to change—change happened. However, progress in raising the profile of the profession continued to be slow until 1993, when the "evangelical accountant" noted above arrived. Sir Andrew Likierman was an academic who "approached his job at the Treasury with an infectious zeal" (Civil Service 2012d) Soon two fundamental changes came about: the first was the decision to introduce accrual accounting; the second, in 1996, turned department finance heads (principal finance officers) from generalists to specialist finance directors, modeled on the private sector. At the time no finance head at the Treasury was an accountant; accountants were still viewed with indifference.

By the time Sir Andrew left his position in 2004, he had persuaded permanent secretaries that all departments should have a professional finance director with a seat on the departmental board. By the end of 2006, all principal finance officers had to be qualified accountants—a recognition of the need for enhanced skills to prepare accrual accounts. Thus, in less than three years departmental spending under the control of a trained accountant moved from 20 to 91 percent. The changes Sir Andrew introduced were driven "hard into the management process."[4] A series of departmental reviews (Cabinet Office 2009), introduced to test how effective Whitehall's financial processes were, identified three main themes for an agenda for change: the decision-making process, the financial skills of senior civil servants, and the quality of the information given to top boards for performance management.

The first of the three led to the Finance Skills for All Programme, a training program developed for government by government to improve the finance skills of all civil servants, whatever their job title. The training is now available in the form of e-learning through Civil Service Learning, a dedicated online portal.[5] It comprises 11 modules from which individuals can select those most relevant to them, their jobs, and their personal development. The modules deal with such areas as financial planning and control, interpretation of accounting data, strategic and business planning, performance indicators, and budget management. General managers throughout the Civil Service were thus required to attain a degree of financial literacy—"managing by numbers." In reality, however, many managers still do not exhibit the level of financial literacy that Sir Andrew envisaged.

Finance heads get together regularly, through numerous events and governance structures, building a network to support each other. For example, monthly government Finance Insight Seminars are held at the Institute for Government, and the Finance Leadership Group meets regularly (the Finance Leadership Group comprises directors general, finance, from all the main Whitehall departments). Senior finance professionals are therefore able to exchange best practices, nurture their careers, and encourage those who wish to follow in their path. The rebranding of the "Government Accounting Profession" as the "Government Finance Profession" was designed to convey the more strategic role its members were to play (Manzoni 2015).

The strategy of recruiting and training more accountants, allied with building up the role of finance as a profession and supported by the heads of profession, began to be reflected in outcomes such as earlier publication of accounts in Parliament: In 2004, 10 departments submitted their accounts to Parliament before the summer parliamentary recess, complying with the good practice outlined in the annual letter from the Treasury Officer of Accounts to Accounting Officers.[6] By 2007, 47 of the 51 departments did so. Meanwhile, a new emphasis on the transparency of external reporting meant that more government estimates and accounts were being published.

The National Audit Office (NAO, annex 1A) was also a significant factor in the drive for timelier and better-quality accounts. The NAO itself had been on a development path, introducing a requirement in the early 1980s that new graduates recruited obtain a professional accountancy qualification. It also invested in training in personal presentation and thinking skills to build confident, persuasive individuals who were more credible to civil servants. The NAO deliberately nurtured a higher profile with the media as part of its role to inform the public. Civil servants increasingly paid attention to auditors' comments and adopted the better practice recommendations in yearend procedures.

Over the years NAO audits identified serious errors and persistent weaknesses in financial reporting, leading to repeated qualifications of a number of accounts (for example, those of the MOD). Meanwhile NAO VfM studies drew attention to the failure of departments to achieve VfM in their management of funds. The PAC hearings based on these VfM reports were often quite critical of departmental activities (NAO 2013b), and the PAC made clear to the public where civil servants were not meeting the expected standards.

The government responded positively to "reports from the NAO and others on our progress, that what we most need is stronger, more effective leadership from the centre to support and strengthen the finance profession across Whitehall for the challenging period ahead. This is in line with our Civil Service reform plan and its call for stronger functional leadership in Whitehall" (Alexander 2013).

Beginning in 1998, spending reviews also projected the future of public services. Expenditure allocations became more directly linked to performance, and the management process was redefined. Resource accounting and budgeting were introduced in 2001. Supporting this drive were measures to reinforce financial management by increasing the number of qualified finance directors and recruiting graduates into the profession via the cross-government Financial Management Development Scheme, although many larger departments also had their own training programs. Over 300 graduates were recruited to this scheme between 2006 and 2012. Trainee and technician numbers grew and diversity improved.

A strong emphasis on governance and accountability underpinned these initiatives. In 2011 the Treasury introduced a new Corporate Governance Code for all departments and rewrote the (original 1915) *Government Accounting Manual*, titling it *Managing Public Money* (annex 1B).

Renewed Political Commitment and the Role and Status of the Finance Profession

In 2011 the then-Government Finance Profession embarked on a "transformational programme" (annex 1C) and launched "Managing Taxpayers Money Wisely: Commitment to Action" (annex 1D). This program had the backing of Justine Greening, then economic secretary to HM Treasury and one of the few ministers to have an accountancy qualification.

This financial management review identified four areas of focus: *people*—ensuring that the right people with the right skills are in the right place; *finance operating model*—a more strategic, efficient, and influential finance function; *data analytics*—ensuring relevant, high-quality, and timely financial data; and *planning and performance*—tools for better financial decision-making. The Finance Transformation Programme (FTP), part of the Civil Service Reform (HM Government 2012), evolved from the recommendations of the Financial Management Review. The FTP aimed to tighten financial discipline and achieve a fundamental shift in public sector culture to make it more commercial, adaptable, and innovative, putting finance at the center of decision-making to protect, improve, and add value for taxpayers.

The Civil Service Reform Plan of June 2012 (annex 1E) gave a further boost to professional skills development. As Sir Bob Kerslake, then head of the Civil Service, said in his Foreword to the Plan, "We will be rigorous about identifying the skills we need, and filling the gaps where we find them. We will focus on professional development and be much better at improving everyone's performance so that all staff can do their jobs better."

In 2013, a government review (annex 1F) of its financial management recommended that the Treasury take action in four areas:

1. *Leadership of Government Finance*
   - Strengthen financial leadership within government by creating a new role, director general for spending and finance, to be responsible for the finance function and overall public spending.

- Strengthen the management relationship between the director general for spending and finance and the Whitehall finance community via a "dotted-line"[7] arrangement to the directors and directors general, finance of the 17 main departments.
- Give greater prominence to the Finance Leadership Group.

2. *Management Information (MI)*
- Invest in ways to better understand the costs of activities and ensure that this understanding is used to better inform decision-making.
- Define standards for costing and MI.
- Continue to build skills across government.
- Accelerate current initiatives to support a common framework, such as adopting the common chart of accounts.

3. *Spending Controls*
- Develop and apply over the medium term a framework within which departments can take more responsibility for some areas of expenditure currently controlled by the center.
- Set a long-term objective of consolidating controls and central government oversight within a single gateway in the Treasury.
- Lead a shorter-term project to better align Treasury and Cabinet Office processes.

4. *Internal Audit*
- Consolidate internal audit shared services over the medium term to provide a single, integrated internal audit service, which will be an independent agency of the Treasury.
- Reinforce the role of the head of profession for internal audit, making it head of government internal audit, reporting to the director general for spending and finance in the Treasury for administrative purposes and with a functional reporting line to the chair of the GIAA Audit Committee. This can become an internal audit service to government departments and to government as a whole. (The GIAA Framework document [2015] provides more details of accountability and operation.)

In response to the review recommendations, the then Government Finance Profession (since renamed the Government Finance Function) set up the Financial Management Reform Programme. This is intended to put finance at the heart of decision making by protecting, driving, and adding value for taxpayers' money (annex 3B). Since 2013, the program has moved from design to implementation, with refreshed governance structures to support its objectives. The five elements of the program are:

- *People*: Developing the staff talent pipeline, all the way through to senior roles.
- *Finance Academy*: Creating solid development opportunities for all in finance, building financial capability and driving continuous improvement.
- *Finance Operating Model*: Sharing expertise across government by creating new Centers of Excellence, stabilizing shared services, and standardizing more processes.
- *Data and MI*: Enhancing how government uses data and MI to improve decision-making, resource allocation, and VfM and ensuring that ministers and senior officials have access to relevant, high- quality, and timely MI.
- *Costing*: Introducing new projects on specific areas of government spending that spans departmental boundaries to get a more detailed understanding of inputs, outputs, and outcomes (Allen and Wolff 2016).[8]

In the Autumn Spending Review (HM Treasury 2015a, 82), the Chancellor committed to "continue to drive up the quality of financial management and the capability of the government finance function to deliver its fiscal plan." The Chief Secretary to the Treasury stated that the "five strand programme is on course and delivering results" (Dunton 2016) and that the program is recognized as the model for delivering change in Whitehall. The Financial Management Reform Program has senior backing from the Finance Leadership Group and is becoming more widely recognized as the platform for driving value and building capability throughout government (Hands 2016).

Progress Reports

In 2013, the government provided an update on progress toward meeting the goals set out in the Civil Service reform effort. The "One Year On Report" (Civil Service 2013b) identified progress in certain areas, such as more up-to-date skills, changing behaviors, the establishment of shared services for financial transactions, and improved management of major projects. But it also identified areas where more work was needed: "Tight public funding means that departments must find ambitious new ways of working to maintain and drive up levels of performance. Key elements of success will be to know what skills are needed and which staff have them, and then deploying those staff to where they are most needed."

Another update a year later indicated that "Progress on the reform agenda has accelerated in the second year of our programme and change is happening on the ground" (Civil Service 2014). For the remainder of 2014–15, work was to focus on the following:

- Cultural change, through issuing a statement making clear the expectations of all leaders in the Civil Service.

- Taking urgent action to fill the critical skills gaps in the Civil Service, particularly digital, project management, and commercial and contract management skills.
- Taking urgent action to remove the barriers that keep talented people from fulfilling their potential, especially the barriers facing under-represented groups.
- Embedding "functional leadership"—"realising the efficiency savings to be gained from the central delivery of cross-government professional services and formalising the role of Heads of Function in leading their profession and raising professional standards. This will be one of the new Chief Executive's core tasks" (Civil Service 2014).

Finance teams in departments and other public bodies have a vital role to play if the government is to reform the public service as planned. In 2013, the NAO noted in its audit report, "Financial Management in Government" (NAO 2013b) that finance managers were being taken more seriously and had a central role in the efforts to provide sustainable services at lower cost. Government tended to operate in silos, limiting opportunities for cost savings. Stronger financial management was needed in departments to speed up the restructuring of service delivery and realize savings.

Success?

There are now almost 10,000 finance professionals[9] in the government, not including devolved administrations, compared with just 500 in 1982. Currently three Permanent Secretaries are qualified finance professionals. All major departments have a qualified finance director with direct responsibility for embedding the Government Finance Profession (GFP) strategy to improve the strength and depth of financial management expertise as it applies to all department budgets. Finance directors are responsible for their teams and for reporting on finance and performance to the senior management board; they do not have a permanent position on the board. The government finance function has defined a model for a Good Finance Director (figure 1.1) that is informed by international best practice and insights from the private sector (Russell 2016, 22).[10]

In recognition of the importance of finance to the management agenda, most departments now have an experienced, qualified director general of finance as a permanent member of the senior management board, alongside directors general of policy and operations. For example, the director general of finance for the Department for Work and Pensions (DWP) is responsible for financial controls and risk management, sourcing and contract/supplier management, resource planning and allocation, and corporate planning and performance management. This suggests that finance is becoming a recognizably high-performing function:

Figure 1.1 The Civil Service's Good Finance Model

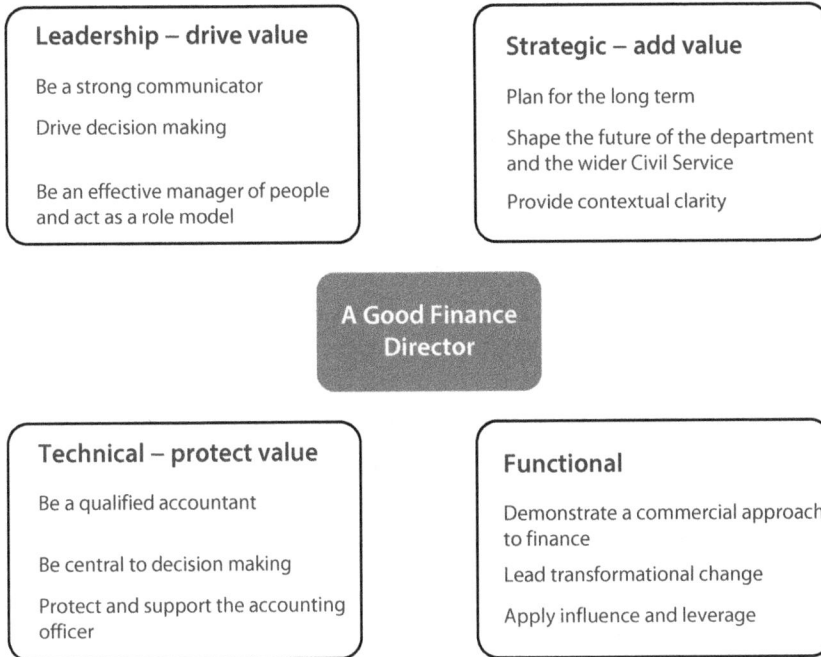

Leadership – drive value

Be a strong communicator

Drive decision making

Be an effective manager of people
and act as a role model

Strategic – add value

Plan for the long term

Shape the future of the department
and the wider Civil Service

Provide contextual clarity

**A Good Finance
Director**

Technical – protect value

Be a qualified accountant

Be central to decision making

Protect and support the accounting
officer

Functional

Demonstrate a commercial approach
to finance

Lead transformational change

Apply influence and leverage

Source: Holmes 2015.

> Conversations in the run-up to the 2015 Spending Review felt different from previous rounds … many more departments had their finance director in the room.… Treasury itself spent more time engaging and supporting and creating the demand and platform for the finance function. (Russell 2016, 22)

There has been significant progress in implementing the recommendations of the 2013 Financial Management Review. According to Russell (2016), "Before the Financial Management Review government finance professionals were viewed as trusted advisers in terms of protecting a department's monetary assets, not as the people to approach for policy insight or programme transformation advice." The review is not seen to be about getting more financially qualified people into government—that is considered to have been achieved. Rather, it is more about how "the finance director can more consistently be the adviser of choice for a Secretary of State or the Chancellor in those moments when key periods of change are happening" (Russell 2016).

Outlook for the Future

The finance profession, which had emerged during the 1980s and made progress in the first decade of the 21st century, moved into high gear when the fiscal crisis hit the U.K. in 2008, bringing sweeping cuts to budgets in local governments, Whitehall, and the public sector as a whole. Policies introduced after the election in 2010 accelerated the change process. After the government's June 2010 spending review, about 66,000 full-time staff left the Civil Service, a headcount reduction of nearly 14 percent (Thomas and Pearson 2014). These were the deepest spending cuts in living memory.

The unprecedented scale and pace of the reforms created huge difficulties for workforce planning: "Whitehall is changing beyond recognition; […] 54,000 staff have been cut from the Civil Service in 18 months, more than was achieved over four years in the 1980s [the last period of downsizing]" (Institute for Government 2012). The largest cuts in absolute terms were made by the three largest departments, although proportionately the smallest departments shrank more (Stephen, Bouchal, and Bull 2013). Some areas of public spending, such as education, are ring-fenced and thus largely protected from these cuts, raising the burden on those with less protection.

In its *Whitehall Monitor 2015*, the Institute for Government noted:

> There were nearly 480,000 civil servants (full-time equivalent) at the 2010 Spending Review; there were just over 406,000 in March 2015, a reduction of 15%. However, the government had expected the Civil Service to be operating with 380,000 staff by 2015, a stark illustration of how difficult any further reductions will be. (Freeguard et al. 2015, 8)

Fiscal Influences

As the U.K. faces severe fiscal pressures, tighter financial discipline is seen as essential to reducing the deficit. A more strategic approach to financial management and a focus on cost-effectiveness are necessary to maintain and improve the quality of all government services.

Spending Reviews in 2010, 2013, and in 2015, identified savings that responded to broader fiscal and economic challenges and outlined plans for total public spending through 2019–20 to ensure that fiscal rules are met (figure 1.2).

- The 2015 Spending Review savings of £12 billion in departmental resource spending by 2019–20 (HM Treasury 2015a, 15) is made up of £21.5 billion of savings from unprotected departments, of which £9.5 billion will be reinvested in government priorities.
- Administration budgets fell by 40 percent from the previous review and will fall by 18 percent more through 2019–20 as the government delivers more for less.

Against the background of year-by-year spending cuts, government is investing in technology to support further improvements in efficiency. The Spending Review 2015 invests £1.8 billion in digital technology and transformation projects across the public sector over the next four years to enable the Government Digital Service to continue to act as the digital, data, and technology center for government, supporting departments as they transform their business operations, setting best practices, and ensuring quality of services.

Figure 1.2 Government Receipts and Expenditure, 2009–21

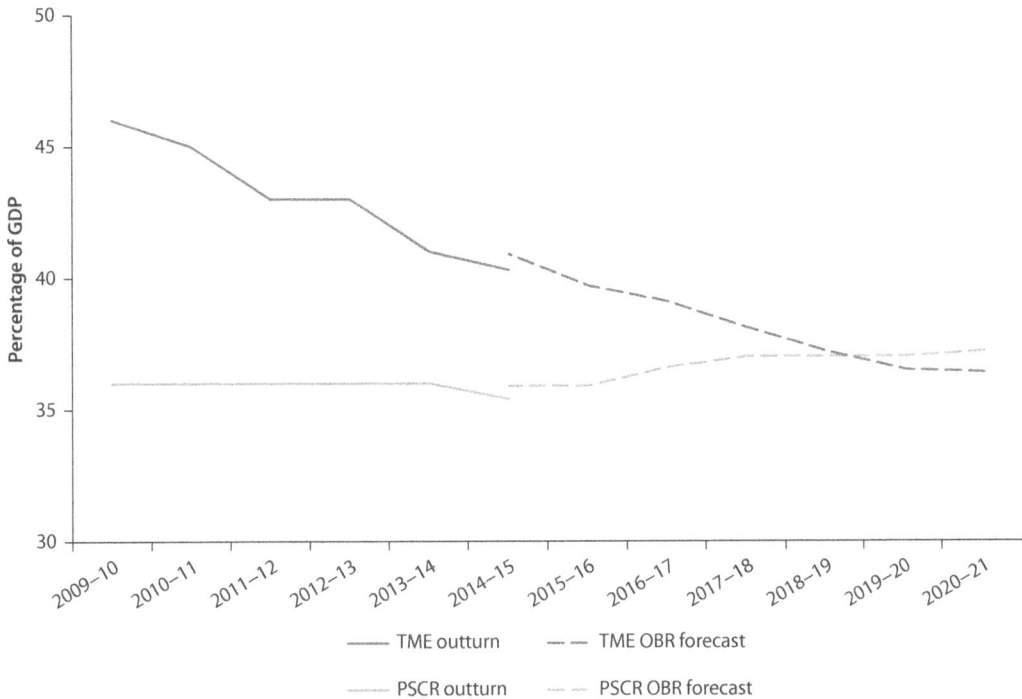

Source: HM Treasury 2015a.

Note: OBR = Office for Budget Responsibility; ONS = Office for National Statistics; PSCR = public sector current receipt; TME = total managed expenditure.

Reshaping the Finance Function's Operating Model

The current U.K. government finance function operating model is complex; it is characterized by a federalized system of finance teams serving a broad range of departments and types of organization. Among government finance leaders there is a clear ambition to move to a more collaborative model where departments share expertise, and the services provided are more consistent and effective. To meet this vision, the finance leadership has agreed to develop an operating model that is:

• Built on more standardized processes and systems, where appropriate and necessary; and
• Seems more "activity delivered" via cross-government shared services and centers of excellence.

To deliver this model there is a new director-led team to act on behalf of the finance function as intelligent customer for shared services, and the government has defined the function's technology requirements and strategy. The director will lead a team of global process owners that is empowered to define and standardize end-to-end government finance processes.

Finance leaders have also agreed to establish by the end of 2016 four centers of excellence for finance—for Costing, Tax, Investment Appraisal, and Technical Accounting—to evaluate the center of excellence model and start to share expertise between departments. This initiative is already underway: seven costing projects have revealed how little awareness there is in departments about how their resources contribute to shared programs. These results have attracted considerable interest and support within Whitehall (Allen and Wolff 2016).[11] HM Treasury will host a full-time costing unit that will have the capacity for 18 zero-based costing reviews of complex policy programs annually and will have the ability to train finance staff in costing—knowledge they can then share with their home departments (Russell 2016).

The cuts have also hit the finance function. Staff numbers have been reduced (see figure 1.3 and table 1.1), partly through redundancy and partly through outsourcing[12]: some more junior transaction processing posts are now part of partnerships with private companies.

Finance staff need more commercial awareness, according to comments by Senior Civil Service (SCS) managers during department self-assessment reviews

Figure 1.3 Number of Finance Function Staff, 2009–15

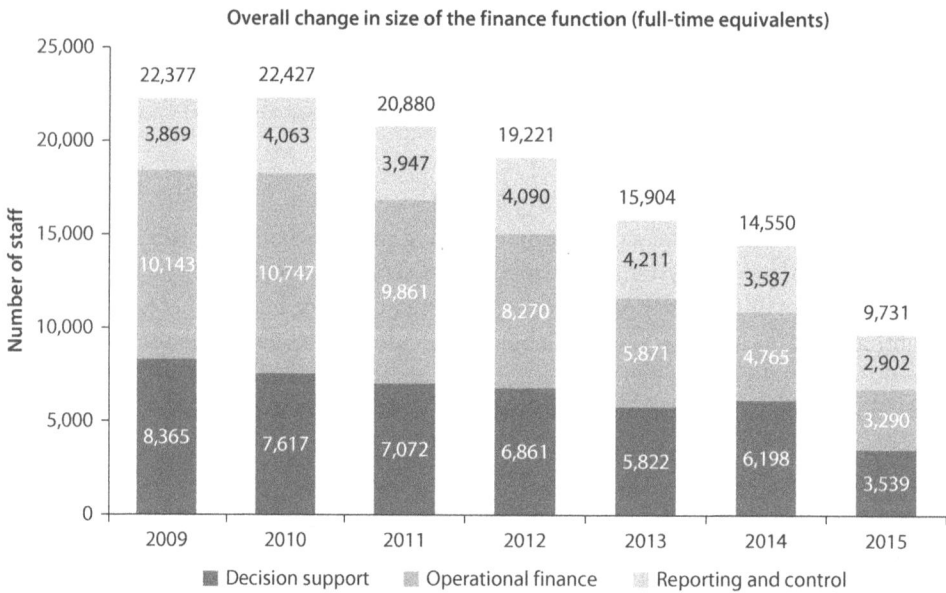

Source: Finance staff survey data, 2009–15, HM Treasury.

Table 1.1 Percentage of Qualified Finance Staff, 2009–15

Year	2009	2010	2011	2012	2013	2014	2015
Percentage of qualified Finance Staff	18	17	19	20	25	27	28

Source: Finance staff survey data, 2009–15, HM Treasury.

for 2013–14. Introducing shared services in itself makes new demands on staff skills. Finance staff will need to manage and monitor these and other contractual relationships. They need to become intelligent customers, adept at negotiations, and, if required, at penalizing poor service. The most significant requirement is for finance staff to be aware that they may need to take a more proactive and timely approach to managing these services.

Although the central government's move to shared financial transaction services has reduced the size of some departmental finance functions, some local governments have taken the concept further. For example, according to a focus group discussion, a large north London Council reduced its core finance function from more than 70 people to 3, two of whom are the director and the deputy director of finance. However, cutting finance too far too fast without first carrying out a good risk assessment may jeopardize the envisaged ability to transform. An organization may need to recruit more sophisticated skills to exploit new technology that is fundamental to transformation. Shared services may make more room to transform finance in the Civil Service but the NAO report on the center of government found that because of resistance from departments to joining them, the shared services centers were not achieving the expected economies of scale (NAO 2014a). It may still be too early to fully assess achievements from this initiative.

To emerge as what the 2015 Spending Review considers a recognizably high-performing function, public financial managers have to leave their comfort zone, acquire new skills, and build their understanding of how the organization delivers front-line services; and operational managers need to remove their protective shields, recognize finance managers as allies who are much, much more than bean-counters, and work with accountants collaboratively.

Move to Collaborative Working

The Treasury is seeking to improve the quality of departmental forecasting. In January 2014, the NAO identified inadequate forecasting as an entrenched problem, leading to poor VfM and higher costs to taxpayers. Part of the problem has to do with data weaknesses—for example, a lack of unit cost information—though departments are now working to acquire more robust data so they can better understand what is driving their costs. Poor forecasts of expenditures as the year progresses often make it difficult for a department to identify over- or underspending and take prompt corrective action. It will be necessary for finance and non finance colleagues, such as policy managers and analysts, to move to more collaborative ways of working (annex 1G), which will help build a better understanding of the data and how they are used.

The Treasury has been working to encourage collaboration between departments. In 2015 it issued a Forecasting and Risk Toolkit to help producers and consumers of forecasts throughout government. Also, an interdepartmental group has been launched to bring together dozens of topic experts and forecast producers across Whitehall to drive continuous improvement. Finally, the Treasury has established a central 1 percent benchmark to drive up forecasting accuracy within departments. This benchmark has improved the conversations between Treasury and departments; about a £2 billion reduction was forecast in 2014–15.

A natural extension of collaborative working that can bring different strands of expertise into the decision-making process is the preparation of plans that cover more than one accounting period. Longer-term planning, typically for three to five years ahead and supported by budgetary controls and effective accountability, would, the NAO believes (NAO 2014a, 7), prove to be a more positive approach to managing spending than traditional central preventive controls. This type of planning offers a "more coherent management of longer-term projects and programmes, which form such a large part of the business of government." Departments are now preparing such medium-term plans.[13]

A factor crucial to recent success (McCrea 2016) was the appointment of the director of the Financial Management Review to run the 2015 Spending Review. The link between the two reviews demonstrated how building up the finance function is essential to delivering the efficiency agenda set out in the Spending Review. The link also illustrates lessons brought into central government based on the previous experience of the Chief Executive of the Civil Service and the Permanent Secretary of the Cabinet Office in managing large multinational organizations. These lessons are now driving the collaboration of different arms of PFM even though each is concerned with different departments, for example, finance for the Treasury and procurement for from the Cabinet Office.

Incentives

The Treasury has announced that "departments demonstrating excellent financial management—including accurate aggregate spending forecasts—would be rewarded with greater budgetary freedoms. In addition, it made changes to the budgetary system to encourage earlier and more transparent forecasting of future underspends." One incentive for departments demonstrating excellent financial management is greater freedom to manage their own resources through higher delegated authorities and greater access to the Budget Exchange scheme, which allows them to carry forward elements of their budget into the following year. For example, having demonstrated good financial management, the MOD was given special dispensation by the Treasury to transfer cash not spent (Blitz 2013) in 2011–12 to 2012–13 and 2013–14. As Philip Dunne, the minister for defense equipment, support and technology, told a reporter,

> By balancing the budget for the first time in a generation, we are now able to prudently protect our underspend thanks to an exceptional agreement with the Treasury so we are ready to fund future priority projects and ensure our armed forces get the equipment they need at the best value for the taxpayer. (Swinford 2014)

The Role of the NAO

Overarching NAO reports on such PFM subjects as internal audit (NAO 2012), forecasting in government (NAO 2014b), and financial management (NAO

2013b) have identified weaknesses throughout government. Also, each year the NAO qualifies certain accounts—such as those of the MOD and the DWP—on the same basis. These critical reports add impetus for improvement.

Other Drivers of Change

Besides offering incentives, the Treasury also wanted to drive change by working with departments to acquire a deeper understanding of departmental financial management capabilities. It therefore required all 17 main departments and their agencies to carry out a financial management self-assessment by the end of March 2015. To encourage consistency, the Finance Leadership Group directed that all departments use a common self-assessment methodology.[14] It was also arranged for Treasury teams to review departmental financial risks and capabilities more regularly.

Positive drivers for change include the move to digital and the allied challenge of "big data." Both these elements require PFM specialists to embrace technical and analytical skills in new ways, and to understand the opportunities to join up and exploit different data sources. For example, with "big data," the DWP can match data from benefit claimants with the HM Revenue and Customs tax database and with local authority databases, in real time, identifying irregularities and potential fraudulent claims. Opportunities are thus available for efficiency savings and a better understanding of costs. The understanding of these opportunities, and the potential for finance staff to use these skills to provide deeper analysis for management, are deemed to be of such critical importance (Civil Service 2014) that organizations (for example, the NAO and DWP) are providing intensive training for their staff on using and exploiting digital technology.

Obstacles to Change

"Implementing the 2015 spending review will be a major challenge for the center" (NAO 2014a), according to the March 2015 Comptroller and Auditor General report. The role of the government finance function is important for spending reviews, but there are a number of impediments to further change. For example, the NAO report, "The Centre of Government: An Update," gives high priority to building capacity in the use of "digital transformation, commercial skills and major projects delivery, along with the capability to manage change." The government finance function in the Treasury and the Crown Commercial Services Group (CCS) in the Cabinet Office are moving to build up skills and capacity in these areas but there is still some way to go.

Another serious problem is aging IT and cumbersome infrastructure. In many departments the information systems are old and unresponsive; presentation of MI is not user-friendly; and after a period of departmental mergers, divorces, and remarriages, some legacy data and interface structure is creaking. To bridge gaps between different financial systems operating within a department, many well-qualified finance staff download data from one system, manipulate them using Excel, and then upload them to another system. This means finance staff have less time to spend on analysis to challenge and support decision-making. Work is underway to address these issues but is not yet complete.

A third issue that has the capacity to slow or even diffuse change already achieved is changes in strategic personnel. "All too often in the past.... Whitehall reforms have failed to embed themselves ... eventually being closed down" (McCrea 2016). Two influential personnel are soon to leave the Treasury, the permanent secretary and the director of public spending. It is necessary that the transition to their successors be smooth if Treasury is to sustain the drive to strengthen PFM and ensure that departments make the changes required. This will require "effective leadership from the centre of government" (NAO 2015).

Annex 1A: The National Audit Office: Helping the Nation Spend Wisely[15]

The National Audit Office (NAO) scrutinizes public spending on behalf of Parliament, helping it to hold government and its departments to account and helping public service managers improve performance and service delivery.

The NAO is central government's external auditor. It has two main aims:

- By reporting the results of its audits to Parliament, the NAO holds government entities to account for the way they use public money, thereby safeguarding the interests of taxpayers (in 2012–13, the NAO audited 437 accounts with spending and revenue amounting to more than £1 trillion).
- NAO's work helps public service managers improve performance and service delivery through about 60 VfM studies a year, examining how government projects, programs, and initiatives are conducted, and how services can be improved.

Independence

- The Comptroller and Auditor General is an officer of the House of Commons. Both he and his staff at the NAO (some 860) are totally independent of government.
- The NAO considers that it can be effective only if it retains the ability to comment objectively and independently on what government does.
- A parliamentary committee, the Public Accounts Commission, oversees the NAO, appoints the NAO's external auditors, and monitors their performance.

Strategic Priorities

NAO's work reveals issues that recur in different government entities; there are three general areas where the NAO has often found a need for improvement. It therefore focuses its output on the following:

- informed government, to encourage government to do more to base its decision-making on reliable, comprehensive, and comparable information;
- financial management, to improve management of activities and encourage the finance function in each department to make its full contribution; and
- implementation, to encourage departments to understand better the key elements in the delivery cycle and what they cost.

Annex 1B: Managing Public Money: Guidance to Civil Servants on How to Handle Public Funds[16]

The public, and Parliament acting on behalf of the public, have a right to expect that funds raised using powers authorized by Parliament will be used for the purposes intended. Public servants have a demanding fiduciary duty to use public money responsibly.

The core of what managing public money requires is just good common sense, sound financial management. There are also some specific rules and conventions about how certain things are handled to ensure that policies, programs, and projects work smoothly and serve their intended purposes.

From the Foreword to *Managing Public Money*:

> Every government needs credibility. Without it, no government can raise the funds it needs for its policies—from taxpayers, from charge payers, or from borrowers. Recent international events have provided object lessons in how fragile sovereign credibility can be.
>
> This handbook helps the U.K. government maintain public trust. It explains how to handle public funds with probity and in the public interest. There is a lot of common sense, with a little protocol about how to respect parliament's requirements.
>
> The origins of this document trace back through the Bill of Rights to Magna Carta. These events brought the monarchs of their day up against the demands of those they governed that the funds they provided should be used wisely. The principles which emerged also underpin the rule of law, for which the U.K. gains international respect and trust.
>
> In modern times it is the elected government that must account to parliament; but the theory is the same. Integrity is the common thread. Transparency and value for public money are the essential results.

The handbook covers all the aspects that trained accountants would expect to help do their jobs well. It is written in an approachable style to ensure that it is read and understood.

The main themes are "the fiduciary duties of those handling public resources to work to high standards of probity; and the need for the public sector to work in harmony with parliament." The handbook reflects the culture and the legal system in the United Kingdom, the principles do not change and the handbook is not, nor should it be, set in stone. It must and should evolve as circumstances—the law, management practices, and public expectations—change. Public sector organizations need to consider new ideas to carry out their responsibilities, using new technology and adopting good business practices.

Parliament expects the government and its public servants to meet the ethical standards set out in *Managing Public Money*, to operate transparently, and to apply common sense!

Annex 1C: Finance Transformation Programme (FTP)

In January 2011, the Treasury set out its intention to deliver a real change in the way public servants manage taxpayer money with the publication of its "foundation" document for FTP: *Managing Taxpayers' Money Wisely* (HM Treasury 2011). The program emphasized the need to strengthen financial discipline; *Managing Taxpayers' Money Wisely* takes this forward, identifying priority areas to be addressed, that is, four enablers of success:

- effective leadership—driving performance from the top;
- cost-conscious culture—every decision is to be built on informed financial assessment;
- professionalism—all public servants need to be financially aware; and
- expert central functions—providing the strategy to work toward common goals.

Also identified were six priority work streams, with leadership for each allocated to a different department to achieve buy-in from departments to the transformation program:

- Finance Capability, led by the DWP
- Finance and Commercial Awareness for Non-Finance Professionals, led by the Ministry of Justice
- VfM and Efficiency, led by the Department for Transport
- Cost Effective Finance Functions, led by Business Innovation and Skills
- Expenditure and Control Frameworks, led by the Home Office
- MI and Reporting, led by the Department for Communities and Local Government.

In June 2013, the Treasury led a review of how to strengthen financial management in government. The review consulted widely with U.K. and overseas finance officials, private sector experts, and finance institutes (Russell 2016).[17] It considered leadership across the finance function, the flow of MI, and the framework of spending controls operated by the center of government. Following the review the Treasury initiated the Financial Management Reform Programme, which superseded the FTP.

The Financial Management Reform Programme has five objectives:

- People: Developing the Civil Service pipeline for getting talented individuals into senior roles.
- Finance Academy: Creating solid development opportunities for all in Finance, building financial capability, and driving continuous improvement.
- Finance Operating Model: Sharing expertise across government by creating four new centers of excellence, taking action to stabilize shared services, and standardizing more processes.
- Data and MI: Enhancing the way all departments use data and MI to improve decision making, resource allocation, and VfM, while ensuring that ministers and senior officials have access to relevant, high-quality, and timely MI.
- Costing: Introducing new projects in specific areas of government spending that span departmental boundaries to acquire a more detailed understanding of inputs, outputs, and outcomes.

Annex 1D: Managing Taxpayers' Money Wisely: Commitment to Action 2011

The U.K. is facing unprecedented fiscal pressures. It has never been more important to take prompt action to embed cost effectiveness and public value in the delivery of all government services. Managing Taxpayers' Money Wisely sets out HM Treasury's intention to deliver a real change in the way that taxpayers' money is managed by public servants. The Programme for Government emphasises the need to strengthen financial discipline; Managing Taxpayers' Money Wisely takes this forward, identifying priority areas that must be addressed: effective leadership, a cost-conscious culture, professionalism and expert central function. (HM Treasury 2011)

This report recognized the significant opportunities the public sector has to learn from the commercial sector, drive value, and improve service to the taxpayer. The government committed to this agenda; it was essential to getting the deficit under control.

To fully exploit these opportunities, it was necessary to transform the public sector culture. Public servants need to manage their financial performance actively, not passively. Decisions need to be evidence-based and have clear financial consequences so that government policies can be implemented with confidence.

The report identified four essential principles:

- Transparency, to provide clear, consistent, comparable, and accessible information.
- Accountability, so that decision-makers and budget holders can be held to account.
- Simplicity, so that it is easy to understand what is going on.
- Coherence, so that government activities are clear and logical.

These, in turn, need enablers to succeed:

- Effective leadership, to drive performance from the top.
- A cost-conscious culture, so that every decision is built on an informed financial assessment.
- Professionalism, so that all public servants are financially aware.
- Expert central functions, to provide the strategy for working toward common goals.

The report views good leadership as the cornerstone of good performance for an effective organization. For the public sector this means the accounting officer and the board need to work in harmony. Nonexecutive board members should provide appropriate support and challenge; the accounting officer and the board must steer their organizations to deliver capability in their fields and manage risks. The government committed to a revised corporate governance code to clarify the roles and responsibilities of boards to support sound financial management. Officials must adhere to CIPFA's core principles for senior finance professionals.

A public organization must build a culture of determined emphasis on sustainable cost reduction. To be effective, budget holders need reliable, timely, and accurate information to plan, organize, and allocate the resources under their control. Civil servants must deliver "more for less and engender a general sense of cost awareness."

The government recognized that to have the quality of information needed to do all of this, a new MI strategy was necessary, supported by simplified frameworks, standard management accounting systems, and processes and behaviors that improve data quality. In addition, how public spending is presented had to be re-thought. In 2009 the government had initiated a reform introducing a "Clear Line of Sight" (HM Treasury 2013a), a means to track individual program elements from budget right through to outturn. Enhancement of mid-year departmental reporting supplemented the expenditure tracking. This would make it easier for the public and the center to hold the executive to account. As this was happening, departments compiled and published integrated operational and financial MI to drive sustainable cost reduction.

Managing Taxpayers' Money Wisely identified the essential need for financial skills to support strategic decisions. Every public service function has a financial aspect that deserves proper assessment and resolution. Financial management should be at the heart of every business decision.

Departments must work through finance professionals, but the report also identifies the SCS as needing to demonstrate a minimum level of capability with financial information and concepts so that they can make responsible corporate decisions. Finance is as much about forward-looking decisions as about accounting for current and past performance. The government requires that all SCS demonstrate a reasonable level of financial competency.

Box A1D.1 Professions of Senior Civil Service Posts as of April 2012

In 2012 there were 3,616 SCS, who constituted 0.78 percent of total Civil Service staff; almost half of the SCS worked in policy. Of the Civil Service professions in the SCS database[a]:

Profession	Number	Profession	Number
Policy	1,055	Procurement	53
Operational delivery	494	Statistics	43
Law	307	Planning	26
Finance	204	Knowledge and information management	15
Project delivery	160	Property and asset management	14
Human resources	123	Internal audit	9
Tax professionals	103	Operational research	8
Information technology	100	Social and market research	8
Economics	80	Veterinarian	8
Medicine	72	Inspector of education and training	6
Communications and marketing	71	Other	90
Science and engineering	69		

Source: Cabinet Office, SCS database.
[a]The numbers of finance staff at SCS level have increased since 2012.

Managing Taxpayers' Money Wisely identifies the need for government to have a sound corporate center to provide strategic direction, mandate minimum operating standards, and provide guidance to departments. Each department should have a small powerful core equipped to bring together its strategic management decisions, which link into the heart of government. The departmental core should consist of experts and become a center of excellence to support the formulation and implementation of strategy and policy, so that it can assess and guide performance.

To help set up and operate this central core, departments need operational metrics for assessing their own performance and understanding where, and how, they should be able to do better. The Treasury is working with the Cabinet Office to define benchmarks, such as balance sheet-related measures like management of working capital. Every department is encouraged to understand and make use of unit cost information to plan more effectively.

Annex 1E: The Civil Service Reform Plan (Civil Service 2012b; Cabinet Office 2014)

The plan covers a number of areas earmarked for reform. This annex looks at the areas influencing future professional development in PFM. As Prime Minister David Cameron said in his Foreword:

The core of the Civil Service Reform Plan is this: harnessing the world-beating talents of those who work in our Civil Service and making sure they aren't held back by a system that can be sclerotic and slow. That means learning from the best in the private sector.

The Future Size and Shape of the Civil Service

The Civil Service will become smaller and more strategic. With 17 main departments, all of different sizes, the government believes that the Civil Service needs a stronger corporate leadership model to enable it to adapt, reform, and emerge from fiscal crises as a much stronger and more agile organization. There will be more sharing of common services (for example, finance, payroll, and procurement) and expertise to increase efficiency to the level required. Sharing services will become the norm. New models for service delivery will be needed to achieve better outcomes or reduce costs. And the Civil Service will transform delivery of services to the end users, moving to a "digital by default" approach.

The plan envisaged a Civil Service that would be about 23 percent smaller in 2015 than it was in March 2010, operating with about 380,000 staff (Stephen, Bouchal, and Bull 2013) in departments ranging from 400 to 80,000 individuals. There are no set targets for headcount reductions; departments must ensure that they are resilient for when they have to embrace change. With a smaller workforce services will have to be delivered differently.

The government reviewed more than 900 public bodies in 2010; the goal of the plan was that by the end of March 2015, about 500 bodies would be reformed and the total number reduced by over 250. The government estimated that there would be administrative savings of £2.6 billion over the spending review period.

The remaining nondepartmental public entities are to be reviewed every three years. The reviews are expected to identify innovations and new models for delivery of public services, such as mutualization and joint venture partnerships with the private sector. They also aim to strengthen accountability and governance arrangements for these entities.

Implementing Policy and Sharpening Accountability

Substantially improve delivery of major projects: The government's past performance on major projects has been poor, with only about a third having been delivered on time and on budget. The reason for much of this failure was that policy is announced before implementation has been fully thought through, and because civil servants have not been given the skills and tools needed for good project management. The government created the Major Projects Authority (MPA) to improve project management and allow delivery issues and failing programs to be exposed early, so that remedial action can be taken before problems mature (Cabinet Office 2015d).

Build a robust cross-government management information (MI) system so that departments can be held to account by their boards, Parliament, the center of government, and the public. The center lacks the good, comparable, accurate, and reliable MI it needs to judge whether departments are achieving. Poor-quality MI also makes it difficult to hold ministers and permanent secretaries to account. MI needs to be improved both within departments and for the whole of government.

Sharpen and make more transparent the responsibility of accounting officers, especially for ensuring that major government projects and programs are conducted effectively, by doing the following:

- requiring explicit accounting officer sign-off on implementation plans, major gateway reviews, and Cabinet Committee papers; and
- establishing the expectation that former accounting officers return to give evidence to select committees, on a time-limited basis, where there is a clear rationale for doing so.

The Role of Nonexecutives

Major reforms to corporate governance introduced 59 high-caliber nonexecutives to enhance departmental boards. New arrangements where secretaries of state chair departmental boards bring together the political and official leadership of departments. For the first time they give nonexecutives and ministers a direct relationship. The role of the nonexecutives is to challenge and support their departments on performance, operational issues (including the operational and delivery implications of policy proposals), and effective management. Many of the nonexecutives previously led large organizations through change and initiated and delivered major projects. They bring a range of skills that are directly relevant to government, particularly considering the major challenges related to reducing the deficit and encouraging growth.

Building up Skills, Deploying Talent, and Improving Organizational Performance

The government identified significant gaps in capability and skills that must be filled if the Civil Service is to meet future challenges. Staff do not believe that their managers are strong enough in leading and managing change. Many more civil servants need commercial and contracting skills as services move further toward a commissioning model (NAO 2009). While finance departments have significantly improved their capabilities, many more civil servants need a higher level of financial knowledge. More rigorous performance management requires that all managers have additional tools and enhanced skills.

Ambitious civil servants tend to gain a range of experience quickly and have short tenures in each post. High turnover in critical posts "can lead to a lack of collective corporate memory and a possible tendency towards orthodoxy" (Civil Service 2012b). As a counterbalance, departments need greater stability of tenure in vital posts.

Government is keen that barriers between the private sector and the Civil Service be broken down to encourage learning between the two. Secondments of staff will help to narrow the cultural gap.

Skills, Learning, and Development
Actions

- *A five-year capabilities plan* is in place for the whole Civil Service to identify in which skills and capabilities there are shortages and outline how the gaps are to be filled. In particular, in a world where more services are commissioned from outside there is a serious need for many more civil servants to have commercial and contracting skills.
- *A new Civil Service Competency Framework* (Cabinet Office 2012) is being used to assess individual performance, identify training needs, draft job descriptions, and assess candidates for vacancies. More consistency is required in applying the framework which could also be more specifically tailored to particular roles.
- *Learning and development* will support the delivery of the capabilities plan and align with the new competency framework. A new Civil Service Learning core curriculum and a learning and development prospectus for all staff have been rolled out and are to be reviewed regularly.
- *Skills in commissioning services.* Many more public servants need skills in managing markets, negotiating and agreeing on contracts, and contract management. A new Commissioning Academy has been established to provide these skills to the whole public sector (NAO 2014c). This is separate from but parallel to the drive to improve procurement practices.
- *The new FTP* is designed to reinforce financial management and give the finance functions in departments and agencies greater authority.
- *Strengthening the authority and influence of the Civil Service professions.* The heads of profession, who operate as cross-government leaders, have an essential role in improving skills and maintaining professional standards. Their role in raising standards, departmental appointments, succession planning, and talent management needs to be given more visibility.
- *Actively managing the Fast Stream*, other high performers, and the SCS as a government–wide corporate talent pool can be done by expanding accelerated development programs, and introducing a single common standard for promotion into and within the SCS. Training for high-potential SCSs can be sourced on the open market through Civil Service Learning, and they can be enrolled alongside high-potential individuals in other sectors, especially the private sector.

The Civil Service One Year On
The next stage of Civil Service reform is directed to more effective support for ministers and greater accountability for the SCS cadre. The goal is to help government deliver better public services and savings for taxpayers.

A Cabinet Office review of the first year of the Civil Service Reform Plan (Civil Service 2013b) identified success in some areas:

- Skills are now more up-to-date. The combination of new intakes of graduates and apprentices, combined with new finance skills for all, is building up skills in all departments.
- Behaviors are changing. A number of departments have introduced initiatives to support changed attitudes and behaviors, for example, the One DWP initiative at the DWP. One DWP operates to foster a more collaborative way of working across the boundaries of professions within the department.
- Services are being shared across government. Progress has been made in bringing together shared transaction services, and other services are converging, as in the establishment of the Government Internal Audit Agency.
- The management of projects is improving. The Cabinet Office has introduced the Major Projects Leadership Academy (MPLA) to support training in procurement and leadership skills, and its work is considered world class. However, much more must be done to manage and reduce turnover of senior responsible officers and put in place effective succession planning to heighten civil service capability to deliver major projects.

Work continues in a number of key areas.

Annex 1F: The Review of Financial Management 2013 and Progress on Recommendations

In 2013 the chancellor and the chief secretary initiated a review of what measures were needed to strengthen government financial management. The review recognized that previous improvements had produced a more confident finance function in many departments; the majority of finance directors now have a professional qualification or a Master of Business Administration (MBA) and sit on departmental boards; and the financial reporting to parliament and the public is clearly better.

Four themes were identified for further improvements in the finance function:

A New Role to Strengthen Leadership in Finance

The position of director general for spending and finance combines leadership of the finance function as a profession with the public spending role. This role, introduced June 2014, provides a defined relationship with the finance function of the 17 main departments through directors and directors general of finance, forming a community of individuals that is a network for discussion and debate. In addition, the Finance Leadership Group will have a higher profile to support the overall structure.

Progress through January 2016: Julian Kelly (CIMA) was appointed as director general of public spending and finance in the Treasury in May 2014 (NAO

2014a). The Finance Leadership Group has been given greater prominence with revised terms of reference to focus in future on talent development and ownership of collective finance and on strategic spending issues (NAO 2014a). Members of the group chair the committees set up to move the Financial Management Reform program forward. (The committees are People, Finance Operating Model, Data and Analytics, Planning and Performance.) Having departmental directors general of finance involved in this way[18] gives the program more traction as the platform for improving financial management across government than would be the case if the program had been imposed from within Treasury.

Management Information

Of vital importance to better decision-making across government is a better understanding of the costs of activities, and what is driving the costs.

Progress: The MI team has agreed on a short-term strategy for improving information and is working to rationalize the MI landscape. It has drawn up a long-term roadmap for improving information for decision making. Work is underway to

- Collate best practices in costing and benchmarking across government. The Treasury is conducting unit costing exercises with departments on which to base a methodology to better support decision-making.
- Incorporate CIMA's Global Management Accounting Principles into finance functions, and assess cross-government best practices in costing on which to base common methodologies and standards.

The first phase of work to align data into a common departmental framework is complete. The Cabinet Office is working with departments to enhance the quality of data and engaging permanent secretaries and finance directors in discussions; discussions have begun on adoption of a common government chart of accounts (NAO 2014a).

Spending Controls

Using a system developed in the center, departments will gradually take responsibility for some spending areas currently controlled by the center. A single Treasury gateway will consolidate controls and provide central government oversight, though this will take time to achieve. Treasury and Cabinet Office processes will be better aligned for a holistic view of spending from decision through reporting.

Progress: Two pilots of a more consistent framework for judging department financial management risk and capability have been completed and are currently being evaluated. The expectation is that the framework will involve regular reviews that draw on a mix of quantitative data and qualitative analysis to arrive at an evidence-based estimate of capability. The Treasury considers that this work will make it easier to target spending controls that reflect department financial management strengths and weaknesses.

The Treasury is reviewing the circumstances in which control for certain spending categories should be transferred back to the Treasury. It is working with the Cabinet Office to understand the implications of the new chief executive for government role.

A project to improve alignment of Treasury and Cabinet Office processes for spending has been completed.

Internal Audit

There is now a central, integrated government internal audit function to serve all departments. The function is an independent agency of the Treasury led by a "head of government internal audit" (also head of profession) as its chief executive, reporting to the director general for spending and finance in the Treasury.

Progress: The Government Internal Audit Agency (GIAA) was launched in October 2014 with the creation of a shadow agency that initially served eight government departments and related arm's-length bodies. Full agency status was achieved on April 1, 2015; the GIAA will ultimately serve at least 13 departments. Negotiation about when it will serve other departments is under-way. New Head of Government Internal Audit Jon Whitfield is in position.[19]

Director General of Public Spending and Finance

For the first time the role of head of public spending is merged with leadership of the government finance function[20]; it will have a formal management link with all departmental heads of finance. The new role will not only strengthen financial leadership in government, it will also be able to drive financial management reforms.

The role will support the director of finance by leading the selection, recruit-ment, deployment, career, and continuing professional development of trainees and finance professionals to ensure that the flow of finance talent meets the needs of the departmental family. It will also act as the finance director's cham-pion in embedding delivery of VfM behaviors as specified in the Civil Service Competency Framework in all relevant grades.

Many departments are choosing to set up deputies where none existed to sup-port the central head of profession and other finance directors within the group.

Features of the Departmental Head of Profession Role

- The post is held in addition to an operational finance post.
- The post holder is given adequate time to fulfill this role,
- Post holders report to the director of finance for this part of their job.
- The post is a key development role for staff wishing to progress within the finance function.

- The post holder works closely with HR, other professions, and other grade managers.
- The post holder is usually a finance professional at one of the three grade gateways.

Annex 1G: Forecasting

Forecasting is an essential component of good financial management and informed decision-making; departments must therefore engender cooperation and understanding between the analysts who produce forecasts and their policy, operational, and finance colleagues who use the forecasts to manage the business (figure A1G.1; NAO 2014b).

Producing and Using Departmental Spending Forecasts

Forecasts inform a range of decisions. For projects and programs, departments use forecasts to make decisions about new investment and whether existing initiatives need to be altered, ended, or resourced from elsewhere. Such forecasts cover projected

- costs, such as the capital expense of building and maintaining a large infrastructure project;
- demand for services;
- staff resources to deliver a service; and
- likely revenue.

Figure A1G.1 Finance and Analyst Collaboration on Forecasting

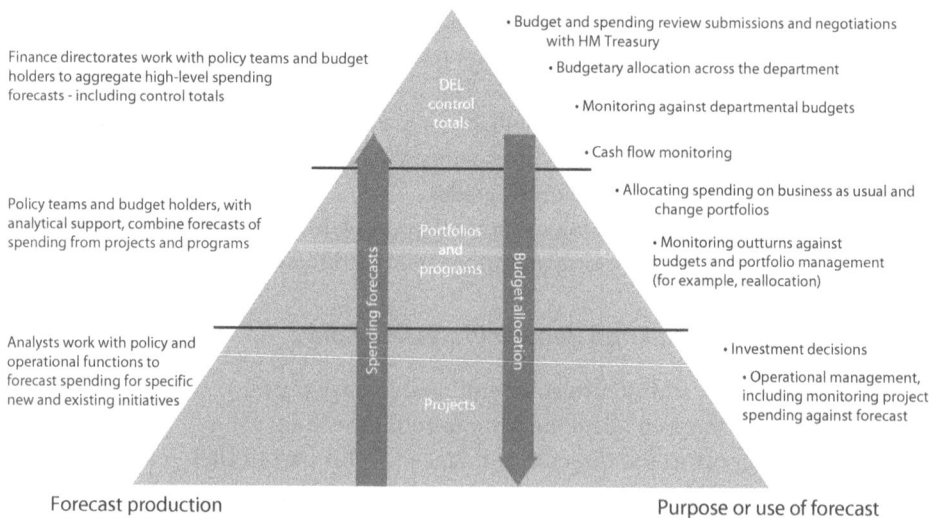

Source: NAO 2014b.

At the aggregate level, departments need to manage their total spending to meet annual budgets. Responsibility for this rests with departmental finance directors and directors general, who participate in project and program decisions and advise boards throughout the year on progress against forecast, such as cash flow, risks of overspending, and scope to reallocate underspends.

Notes

1. The Public Accounts Committee (PAC) is the oldest select committee in the House of Commons. The committee examines accounts laid before Parliament and reports produced by the Comptroller and Auditor General (C&AG) on value for money (VfM) studies of economy, efficiency, and effectiveness.

2. John Codling, previously Department for Work and Pensions (DWP), quoted in The Early Years: 1968 to 1982, Government Finance Profession in association with Chartered Institute of Management Accountants (CIMA) 2012.

3. Head of Accountancy Profession was later re-titled Head of Finance Profession.

4. Mary Keegan, quoted in The Early Years: 1968 to 1982, Government Finance Profession in association with CIMA 2012.

5. Since April 2012, Civil Service Learning has bought and supplied generic skills training for the entire civil service, replacing a system under which individual departments procured their own. The reform saves the government c. £80m a year through economies of scale, reduced duplication, and a shift to digital training. http://www.global-governmentforum.com/interview-jerry-arnott-former-chief-executive-civil-service-learning-U.K.

6. All departments have a statutory requirement to publish their accounts; departments are given also a statutory deadline by which they are required to submit accounts to the Comptroller and Auditor General. For 2013–14 the deadline for the Comptroller and Auditor General was November 2014.

7. The dotted-line arrangement here provides professional oversight and supports a collaborative relationship rather than the direct accountability attributed to straight-line reporting arrangements.

8. The costing reviews take a whole-system approach to services delivered across organizations to break down silos. The reviews increase understanding of costs and opportunities for benchmarking and find smarter ways of working.

9. This figure relates to core finance, such as accounts, rather than the broader group of individuals working in public financial management (PFM).

10. This model reflects traditional abilities as well as building in the ability to lead across organizational boundaries, how to work on a management board and demonstrate strategic thinking and commercial know-how.

11. The article discusses some of the issues that the costing projects have revealed about what drives efficiency. For example, one of the findings from the costing projects suggests "that placing hard budget constraints can increase efficiency," though there does not seem to be one single key driver.

12. For a discussion of shared services in the public sector, see "Innovation in the Back Office," https://www- 304.ibm.com/easyaccess/fileserve?contentid=223691.

13. Self-Assessment Reviews of Financial Management in Departments facilitated by CIPFA, using their FM Model, and HM Treasury comment February 2016.

14. Letter to Departments from Head of Government Finance Profession February 2013. CIPFA FM Model was used as a diagnostic toolkit for the self-assessment reviews. The FM Model can be used to identify efficiency gains and pinpoint strengths and weaknesses in financial management.

15. https://www.nao.org

16. https://www.gov.U.K./government/publications/managing-public-money

17. The review drew particularly on the expertise of a board whose members included the chief finance officers of BP, Unilever, and Vodaphone.

18. Departmental finance heads carry out reviews and identify recommendations to support their subject committee and in doing so involve finance staff from across government. "This bottom-up approach should lead to a programme that is more tailored to departments' need" (NAO 2014a).

19. Progress against recommendations in the Financial Management Review, provided by HM Treasury to PAC in October 2014.

20. https://www.gov.U.K./government/news/new-director-general-of-public-spending-and-finance-appointed. The creation of this new role was a recommendation of the Financial Management Review (FMR), launched at Spending Round 2013.

CHAPTER 2

Organizational Framework

Network, Responsibilities, Capacity, and Effectiveness

In the Civil Service, a wide range of professionals are mapped to 25 recognized professions (Civil Service, n.d. b). Professional leadership of eight of these business areas—including commercial services (procurement and project management), internal audit, and finance—is bolstered through a functional, centralized leadership program. The government intends to embed the functional leadership role to "realise the efficiency savings to be gained from central delivery of cross-government services; and formalise the role of Heads of Function in leading their profession and raising professional standards" (Civil Service 2014).[1] This "functional model" is expected to retain sufficient flexibility to allow collaboration between functions and areas where it is considered sensible to do so (Manzoni 2015).

- *Finance function*: After a Financial Management Review in June 2013, a new director general of public spending and finance (DGPS) (annex 1F) was announced. This position combined director general of public spending with being head of the government finance function. In the latter role, the DGPS oversees the selection and career development of directors and directors general of finance for all departments. The DGPS supports the department directors general of finance by leading selection, recruitment, deployment, performance assessment, career, and continuing professional development of trainees and finance professionals. This position thus ensures that the flow of finance talent meets the department's business needs. The management relationship between the DGPS and department finance directors is being more closely linked: the DGPS will provide input into finance director appraisal discussions, based on their compliance with financial policies set by the center and their cooperation on cross-cutting finance matters. Departmental directors and directors general continue to report to their permanent secretaries on routine issues and delivery of departmental strategy.

- **Internal audit function**: Staff are supported in their work by the Audit and Assurance Policy Team, which has been part of the the Government Internal Audit Agency (GIAA) since April 2015 (annex 2A). This team sets standards and policies, formulates good practice guidance, and provides learning and development opportunities. Internal audit staff were previously dispersed among several shared service groups serving government departments. The heads of internal audit in those groups previously had local, day-to-day responsibility for training and development and guidance for their staff. In October 2014, internal audit teams began to move into a single shared-service agency, reporting to the Treasury head of public spending though an independent agent of the Treasury, as envisaged in the Civil Service reform. Full executive agency status for the GIAA took effect in April 2015. The goal is for the service to ultimately cover at least 13 departments, as well as many nonministerial departments and arm's-length bodies (HM Treasury 2014).[2] The GIAA is developing as it grows, and inevitably with such a previous geographic spread, consistency in the quality of departmental and agency reporting has yet to be achieved.
- **Procurement function**: The procurement function is in the remit of the Crown Commercial Services (CCS), which is part of the Cabinet Office (annex 2B). The CCS is responsible for rolling out training across central government to support new developments in the profession.
- **Project delivery function**: This is an informal network for civil servants who work in, or are involved with, projects (annex 2C). *Project delivery* is an umbrella term covering the support, management, and leadership of projects, programs, and corporate delivery portfolios. This function is vital to successful implementation of government policy and organizational change in the public sector. It has set up a project delivery curriculum for staff that blends work-based, online, and classroom learning in line with the best practices of top-performing public and private organizations.
- **External audit**: The National Audit Office (NAO) (annex 1A) is not part of the Civil Service. As an independent organization it makes its own arrangements for training. There are several streams of audit work (referred to as a "fan of assurance" [Public Accounts Commission 2014]), including financial and value for money (VfM) audits; each has its own training route. For financial audit, auditors are recruited to train (usually) in the Institute of Chartered Accountants in England and Wales (ICAEW); for VfM studies, a variety of professions and other backgrounds are represented—there is no single training body.
- **Analyst professional group** (especially economists and statisticians): These staff contribute to forecasting and planning. Although not considered part of the core functional groupings within public financial management (PFM), they are vital collaborative partners facilitating its strength and sustainability.

Professional Qualification Civil servants in the core PFM professions are required to train in an appropriate qualification from a recognized professional institute or training entity. A university degree is not considered sufficient on its own to carry out the function effectively, although certain courses within the degree may provide either exemption from or credits toward a professional qualification. Economists and statisticians who have no obvious professional institute qualification are encouraged to gain strong subject skills by pursuing further degrees, taking short specialist training, and joining relevant networks.

- *Finance function*: There are four main professional institutes in England and Wales (annex 2D)[3]: Chartered Association of Certified Accountants (ACCA); Chartered Institute of Management Accountants (CIMA); Chartered Institute of Public Finance and Accountancy (CIPFA); and ICAEW. Three of the institutes focus on the private sector, though they also have some students from the public sector; all share some commonality with regard to their syllabi. Entry into the Civil Service training in these finance qualifications normally requires that entrants have a university degree or a qualification with the Association of Accounting Technicians (AAT).[4]
- In a new scheme started in 2013 to attract school leavers to the finance function, initial entry is through AAT apprenticeship training (annex 2E). The new scheme is directed to those who do not wish to pursue a degree but who are clear that they wish to be finance professionals. Success in the AAT exams allows students to progress into the main professional institutes for the finance function.
- *Internal audit*: The Chartered Institute of Internal Auditors (CIIA, annex 2F) is the only institute dedicated to awarding internal audit qualifications and training internal audit staff. Finance professionals qualified with the accountancy and finance bodies described are also qualified to carry out internal audit work.
- *Procurement*: The core qualification institute in the U.K. for procurement is the Chartered Institute of Purchasing and Supply (CIPS; annex 2G). The institute is working with the procurement function in the Cabinet Office to draw up a curriculum tailored to the needs of government procurement.
- *Project delivery function*: There are two common training approaches for project management, both short, high-intensity courses: the qualification offered by the Association of Project Managers and training in PRINCE2. The specific qualifications, however, depend on the position requirements and the project methodologies used.

Many other professional qualifications are available (such as treasury management, risk management, counter-fraud; annex 2H) to complement those discussed. Most are relatively short specialist courses. Ultimately, Civil Service professionals must each take responsibility for their own training and development needs (Civil Service 2013a).

Civil Service Human Resources, one of the core functions (Civil Service n.d. a), consists of a number of different expert services. It is relevant to mention here because it includes CS Learning, which provides, among other things, a range of basic finance, risk management, and governance courses—resources for building the skills common to all U.K. civil servants in all functions—and can add courses upon request.

All ministries, departments, and other Civil Service bodies use a new HR Talent Toolkit (annex 2I) created by the Civil Service for building talent management. This toolkit helps departments to better plan the future development and deployment of PFM staff.

The government finance function is managed by the Finance Capability team, based in HM Treasury. It crafts and oversees implementation of strategies for improving financial management across central government, in particular the financial management reform program. The team also maintains a website, accessible only to Civil Service employees, for coordinating and disseminating information to support finance professionals—for example, details of conferences and other learning and development events, and news and information from the various professional institutes.

In the finance area of every department a local head of profession provides continual professional support, training, and development advice to finance staff. How active departmental heads of profession are is somewhat dependent on departmental culture and the character of the individual concerned. Proactive heads act as mentors to staff that are new to finance and draw up a diary of training and development activities ranging from technical seminars to short tailored training courses. Heads may also provide guidance on application of the competency framework for drafting local job descriptions, carrying out annual performance appraisals, and identifying development opportunities for individuals in the department—for example, an experienced and capable finance professional might spend a week experiencing front-line service delivery.

The Treasury and Cabinet Office Administration budgets fund centralized functions such as the core government finance function. The finance function carries out a range of events—for example, an annual conference—to support development of the profession across the government. Departments also undertake work to build the capability of the finance function and profession.

For more senior civil servants holding responsible roles in project delivery, the Major Projects Authority (MPA)—part of a new organization, the Infrastructure and Projects Authority (IPA), since January 1, 2016—established the Major Projects Leadership Academy (MPLA) to help build leadership for complex major projects. The academy is sited at Saïd Business School, part of Oxford University.

However, identifying networks and providing professional training are not sufficient in themselves to establish a sustainable movement to transform a profession:

> The real challenge is to shift the long-standing culture in the civil service to create a leadership group with the full range of skills needed for success, today and in the future, that is a shared resource across government. This is far easier said than done. The case for a corporate approach is now inescapable but achieving full buy-in

from departments will take time. Progress will need to be rapid and involve all senior civil servants, not just those on corporate talent programs. (NAO 2013a)

Training Providers

A number of training providers are available for each professional qualification. Providers offer a mix of training types, such as classroom, e-learning, online learning, and distance learning.[5] Sometimes students select a qualification; in others, the department chooses for them. Students choose the type of learning and the provider. Some students find training in a classroom format challenging once they have left university but others prefer the discipline that this brings; for those who have family commitments, distance or e-learning is a more achievable option.

The institutes maintain lists of approved or accredited providers on their websites, where they also define their accreditation criteria; to be accredited, a training provider must demonstrate that it meets the criteria. Approved and accredited training providers maintain documentary evidence of their own training and experience. An institute visits the provider from time to time and may examine the evidence during the visit. According to the ICAEW, providers may, and do, lose accreditation. It can be expensive to qualify and maintain accreditation because qualified staff must visit providers across the country.

Training providers are mainly from the private sector, though a few universities and colleges also provide training. The market is dominated by a small number of large countrywide providers of accountancy, finance, and internal audit training (for example, Kaplan, Brierley Price Prior, and the Institute of Internal Audit [IIA]), which train for all the professional finance and chartered internal audit exams. CIPFA and Kaplan have trainers with specific public sector experience, though not necessarily experience with the central government. There is also a wide range of training providers for procurement and project management qualifications—including, for project management particularly, universities.

The syllabus for each professional qualification is available on the Internet. The institutes offer their qualifications in stages, which allow individual students to take time away from study; it is possible to gain certificates or diplomas without pursuing the full route to qualification. Most training qualifications, like degrees, must be completed within a set number of years. Institutes also offer shorter, specialized qualifications to complement the core qualification.

Syllabi are very detailed; courses are often made up of subject modules. In finance and accountancy, certain core modules are common to all professional accountancy qualifications (for example, financial management); other modules are common to accountancy and audit, or even accountancy, audit, and procurement. Each institute defines its core modules, the content of the modules, and the part they play (sometimes in terms of credits) in building toward the overall qualification. At the more advanced levels of many qualification routes, students may select options for study from a list.

ACCA allow exemptions to their Fundamentals and Foundation levels for relevant qualifications studied elsewhere; ACCA and Oxford Brookes University worked together to develop a BSc (Hons) degree in applied accounting, which is available exclusively to ACCA students who wish to obtain a degree while studying toward the ACCA Qualification. The ACCA qualification therefore provides exemptions toward the Oxford Brookes BSc degree. The two are mutually beneficial; students have the opportunity for a fast track route to a degree.[6] Exemptions may also be offered for students who have passed certain exams with another training body. Exemptions are not guaranteed.

ACCA, CIMA, and ICAEW provide the same courses for students from the public and the private sector; these courses tend not to cover public-sector-oriented content. The courses run by CIPFA are dedicated to the public sector. Each finance or accountancy institute has its own criteria for training. Enrollment in most of the accountancy institutes tends to be consistent from year to year across all sectors, although CIMA's intake has continued to grow (see table 2.1).

- **ACCA** encourages diversity; to offer opportunities for all, it has no set entry requirements except that the students be numerate. The institute recognizes that, as a result, the failure rate on its exams is higher than that in other institutes (for example, ICAEW). About 12 percent of ACCA members worldwide work in the public sector (FRC 2015b); and two-thirds of those working for government in the U.K. are in the health sector. ACCA believes its qualification is attractive to students because it is portable across sectors.
- **CIMA** traditionally has been closely associated with industry, and its syllabus focuses on management accounting and business practices. CIMA believes one strength of its training approach is that it too encourages portability of good practice across private and public sectors. The Health Services and the MOD previously gave priority to CIMA training for staff. Some 10–15 percent of CIMA members worldwide work in the public sector (FRC 2015b).
- **CIPFA** is the only institute to train only for the public sector. It provides a varied program in cooperation with other awarding bodies, such as the Treasury Management Institute. CIPFA has a role in promoting public finance globally and in developing accounting and audit standards for the public sector (it offers a diploma in international public sector standards). It also provides short training events tailored to the specific needs of certain groups, for example, courses for the police or local authorities, and to address issues of specific public sector concern, for example, performance and efficiency

Table 2.1 Number of Finance Graduates, 2013

Institute	Number of Graduates
ACCA	11
CIMA	25
CIPFA	12
ICAEW	11

Source: Reply to a parliamentary question.

improvement and public sector reform. About 62 percent of CIPFA members worldwide work in the public sector (FRC 2015b).

- **ICAEW** has traditionally been closely associated with the private sector, with some 30 percent in public practice, mainly in accountancy firms; worldwide less than 10 percent of ICAEW members work in the public sector. However, ICAEW also considers the portability of its qualification to be attractive (FRC 2015b). The NAO trains its financial audit staff in the ICAEW qualification, which is closely associated with auditing. ICAEW is a relatively new qualification for individuals training and employed outside of a recognized audit firm or the NAO. A department wishing to support students studying with ICAEW needs to become an authorized training employer, a free and straightforward process; to date ICAEW has accredited nine government organizations in addition to NAO (Civil Service n.d. c).
- **The CIIA** qualification allows members to move out of audit into the business of the organization. Potentially this approach offers a route to disseminate good internal control practice throughout the organization while giving students a good overview of the whole business from within the audit role.
- The government procurement profession is working with the **CIPS** to customize a program of training to the needs of the government.
- The project delivery profession is working closely with **Saïd Business School at Oxford University** and **Deloitte** to provide specialized leadership training (the MPLA) for those assigned to major projects.

For any of these qualifications, most classroom training is for mixed groups of public and private sector students, or in the case of CIPFA from different parts of the public sector. Classroom teaching requires a record of attendance, so training providers, employers, and training institutes record the numbers of students attending. Some departments ask providers like Kaplan to train employer-focused groups of students. This approach has advantages and disadvantages: students from one employer feel confident in studying together and form a strong network, providing mutual support as they progress through their careers; however, mixed groups of students from both public and private sectors offer the opportunity to learn good practice in different sectors and bring that back into the employing organization.

Self-guided e-learning is becoming more popular, but the costs of creating study materials may be high. There is some anecdotal evidence that students choosing to pursue e-learning are more likely not to complete the course than those choosing traditional routes. Online learning is a live learning option: students can log in and take part in a virtual classroom, with a tutor leading the study period. It can be a useful option when there are likely to be language difficulties, as groups with a common language can be formed from a distance.

The duration of training varies according to the institute and the type of training. For the accountancy and finance institutes, qualification usually takes at least three years. Students formally qualify when a training record of their work experience is verified by a signature from their employer. The record must include the student's reflections on the learning experience. The record may be subject to an institute assessment or other check, such as a meeting with the employer. For the AAT, duration of training depends on the student's level when training begins. Qualification with the CIIA takes a little less time than with the accountancy institutes. Qualifying with CIPS takes about 250 hours of e-learning spread over a period during which the candidate also acquires relevant work experience. The MPLA program takes a few days of study combined with learning in the role.

On joining a government department, all trainees in the professional streams are assigned a mentor (annex 2K) and a training buddy. The departmental head of profession provides general oversight and support.

In January 2016, the government finance function launched a Finance Academy to provide coherent learning and development opportunities for people working across the finance function. The launch focused on priority areas for the government finance function: Finance Business Partnering, Commercial, and Technical (on such subjects as tax and data visualization[7]). The academy also has career pathways to help civil servants plan particular trajectories in government finance, setting out the skills and experiences required to fulfill identified core roles.

Annex 2A: Internal Audit Function

The U.K. spends an estimated £60 million on internal audits for central government. These operations entail about 800 in-house staff and 125 full-time equivalent contractors, who provide £13 million in internal audit services. About 82 percent of Internal Audit staff are professionally qualified (CMIIA, Consultative Committee of Accountancy Bodies [CCAB] [http://www.ccab.org.U.K.], or equivalent).

Internal Audit provides an independent and objective assurance to the most senior management of about 450 public entities that their systems and controls are fit for purpose. That assurance should cover financial and operational controls for core systems, governance, and risk management processes. At the heart of this governance work is assurance of management control of the quality of the information, which the accounting officer, the board, and the entire business use to make decisions and monitor performance (NAO 2012).

HM Treasury, which requires that all central government bodies have an internal audit function, is responsible for setting standards and policies for internal audits (NAO 2012). The NAO (2012) review of internal audit of central government as a whole found that "Government was not getting the most out of the £70 million it spends on internal audit because the service does not always focus on the right issues and it is often not of sufficient quality to be useful in decision-making" (NAO 2012).

> Users of internal audit identified particular gaps in such areas as the usefulness and relevance of reports; the expertise of staff, including expertise in IT-based information systems; the identification of efficiencies in the organization; and the ability

to offer advice to senior management. Some 40 per cent of stakeholders thought some or substantial improvement was needed in the expertise or professionalism of internal audit. (NAO 2012, 23)

In parallel with the financial management review (HM Treasury 2013b), the Treasury reviewed the functional leadership of the government's internal audit service. The review recommended moving from disparate audit groups (10 teams serving 17 departments) to a single integrated internal audit function. The new cross-departmental service is designed to do the following:

- consolidate internal audit shared services over the medium term, providing a single, integrated service as an independent agency of the Treasury;
- build up the role of the head of profession for internal audit, making the job title head of government internal audit, reporting to the Treasury director general for spending and finance; and
- serve both individual departments and the government as a whole.

The government's internal audit service is particularly important for supporting transformation in the application of financial management practices, as well as all other aspects of government activity. The shared services are being consolidated into a single integrated government internal audit service, the GIAA (GIAA 2016b). This move is designed to maximize the benefits from sharing resources, specialist skills, and talent while continuing to provide high-quality, responsive, and flexible service to each department. It will also reinforce moves to identify and manage a cross-government view of risk and assurance. The integrated service will establish new reporting lines, such as that of the new function, head of government internal audit. A decision has yet to be made about other government organizations (HM Treasury 2014).

The single government internal audit service will provide the following:

- a comprehensive and flexible service dedicated to and agreed with accounting officers and their audit and risk assurance committees to support them in managing their departmental and arms'-length board delivery and other risks;
- a framework for escalating recognition of significant local risks, especially those that may have broad impact on the government;
- a service to the center of government to provide assurance explicitly on cross-government risks and common performance measures.

In addition to overseeing cross-government operational elements, the head of government internal audit will take a holistic view of resource requirements and capabilities across the field. Heads of internal audit reporting to individual departments from within the GIAA will be accountable to the head of government audit, who will be responsible for maintaining a single set of detailed professional standards and driving continuous improvement.

The New Service

The GIAA is considering a rotation policy for its staff (perhaps 30 percent will move every three years) to refresh and develop their skills. The downside of this policy is the difficulty of maintaining continuity and client knowledge to ensure an efficient audit. Customers are concerned to retain a service tailored to their entity rather than the service becoming a uniform product. On the other hand, according to the deputy head of GIAA, rotation offers opportunities to more easily share good practice and possibly support benchmarking.

In 2014–15 there were two Fast Stream graduate entrants with the GIAA, which currently has 180 staff. Previously each internal audit group recruited its own staff; in future recruitment will be centralized.

The new agency will have a central pay scale rather than the previous local rates. Currently, internal auditors may gain up to an extra £8,000 for earning the auditor qualification, though the norm is about £5,000 (below the Senior Civil Service [SCS] level). Though now there are different terms for the audit allowance, depending on the department, this will change. Staff members who move out of internal audit usually lose their professional payment.

It is not easy to compare private and public sector pay for internal auditors; the private sector does not tend to recruit to this level of expertise, nor in such numbers. In the private sector most internal auditors are accountants, which is not currently the case in the public sector. The service intends to formulate a talent management policy but it not quite there yet. As a new organization the GIAA has not yet finalized a training budget.

Training and Qualification of Internal Auditors

Internal audit job opportunities arise often. Depending on the post, an individual may be able to train from scratch or may need to possess an internal audit or accountancy qualification. Other qualifications can be extremely valuable; the work is varied, challenging, and draws upon a broad range of skills.

There is no preferred supplier of professional training for the internal audit function, but three potential suppliers have been identified. Individuals can obtain their training directly from the Chartered Institute of Internal Auditors (CIIA) or (more commonly) from its approved provider, Birmingham City University Business School, or BHBi All internal auditors must attend an induction course for auditors in government. The GIAA is considering other short courses for internal auditors, and in future the agency may work toward a common training provider. In making any decision it will need to be careful not to skew supply to one area. Currently there are several routes into the internal audit profession:

1. Individuals who are qualified in whole or in part with a professional CCAB institute, such as Chartered Institute of Public Finance and Accountancy (CIPFA), or hold CIIA status can apply for a vacancy as an external candidate. Partly qualified individuals are often supported to complete their stud-

ies or offered an opportunity to study for CIIA. Some individuals with CCAB qualifications choose to add the CIIA qualification, but this is not a requirement.

2. During the GIAA move to full agency status in April 2015, and while decisions are still to be made on providing internal audit to other government organizations, new candidates to the profession may apply to join internal audit through a central or local vacancy, through the new internal audit Fast Stream graduate entry scheme (following the core Fast Stream application process), or through the Fast Stream apprenticeship scheme. For organizations not yet covered by the GIAA, the local head of internal audit and the individual may decide together which training qualification is selected, or there may be a local preference for a particular qualification.

3. Internal candidates not currently in Internal Audit may apply for internal audit vacancies if they are

   a. a staff member with a financial qualification who is seeking a career move;

   b. a trainee in the finance department who wishes to transfer to internal audit; or

   c. a member of the nonfinancial staff who wishes to change careers and will start training within internal audit.

Vacancies are filled on merit.

For the first year, a new entrant is based in Internal Audit. Trainee will then undertake a series of 6- to 9- month postings to other areas of their departments, for example, risk management, finance, or IT services. Experience will be broadened through placements in different government departments and professions. There are several routes into general auditing and one into IT auditing. Trainees will be supported to achieve professional qualification with the CIIA, the CCAB, or an equivalent entity as well as specialist qualifications, such as the Certified Information Systems Auditor certification from the Information Systems Audit and Control Association.

Though specialist skills, such as contract audit, are often required, they may be provided by a short-term contractor or by a career move from procurement.

Competency: Currently internal audit groups use the generic Civil Service Competency Framework (Civil Service 2012a); a linked Internal Audit Profession Competency Framework is being developed. The individual and the head of internal audit agree on a development program based on the competency framework. Development may include further formal training or a placement in another function, such as procurement.

Annex 2B: The Procurement Function

The Civil Service Procurement Profession is "an informal network for civil servants who work in, or are involved with, procurement for government" (Civil Service n.d. d). These professionals work in both the central government

Procurement Service and in departmental centers of commercial excellence. The Procurement Service is part of the Crown Commercial Services (CCS), which together with the commercial function of the Cabinet Office forms an Executive Agency of the Cabinet Office. The head of the CCS is head of the government procurement profession.

In 2013, the central government spent about £45 billion on goods and service; the public sector as a whole spent £227 billion (Civil Service 2013a). The CCS aims to act as a single customer, buying essentials for the whole of government in the most efficient way possible and freeing departments to focus their procurement expertise on needs that are unique to them.

Driver for Change in Procurement

In its critical 2013 report, "Meeting the Challenge of Change," the Public Administration Select Committee stated:

> There are clear shortcomings in the ability of the Civil Service to run effective and efficient procurement. The Civil Service shows a consistent lack of understanding about how to gather requirements, evaluate supplier capabilities, develop relationships or specify outcomes. We welcome the initiatives to improve capability and skills, such as the Major Projects Leadership Academy and those set out in the Civil Service Reform Capabilities Plan, but a more fundamental shift is required. Little is known about the skills and experience or lack thereof of 17 of the 61 senior procurement civil servants across Whitehall, and consequently there is little coordination of this vital resource.
>
> The government has initiated steps to improve the efficiency and effectiveness of government procurement: improving its data, aggregating demand across government departments, and renegotiating the relationship with major suppliers. The stream of procurement and contract management failures, however, continues unabated. (Civil Service 2013a)

Further criticism of procurement and of the related professional activity "delivery of major projects" was directed at several major projects, notably the innovative but complex Universal Credits project in the DWP.

Excellent procurement is fundamental to deficit reduction and economic growth. The Cabinet Office believes that this contribution can only be maximized if the capability of government procurement professionals is continuously recognized, valued, and improved. It recognizes that value for money in procurement will only be achieved if civil servants have the right specialist capabilities. But commercial activities encompass more than just procurement; and a requirement for commercial capability is not restricted to those engaged in commercial activities. Achieving Commercial Outcomes is a core Civil Service competency (Civil Service 2012a), and commercial learning and development is part of the Civil Service Learning curriculum.

The Capabilities Plan aims for all civil servants involved in policy development to be more commercially astute, maximizing value during all three phases of commercial engagement—pre-procurement, procurement, and post-contract. In effect the government want to restack the commercial balance in dealing with suppliers.

Procurement Training and Development

According to the government's chief procurement officer, Bill Crothers, CCS head (2015), "Continuous professional development and improving commercial capability sits at the heart of Civil Service Reform and the Capabilities Plan."

Procurement professionals have a range of duties, among them engaging with suppliers to shape requirements, drawing up commercial procurement strategies, running a lean procurement process, managing contracts, settling disputes, disposing of assets, and re-competing for a service.

Improving the capability and confidence of procurement staff is critical to the success of the government procurement reform strategy and at the heart of the Procurement Profession. For those already working in procurement or commerce who would like to build their procurement skills, the CCS offers training for staff in central government and in the public sector as a whole. A list of short training courses is available on the CCS website (CCS 2014b).

In 2015, a new Commercial Fast Stream Graduate Scheme was launched as part of an ambitious program to raise government commercial capability generally (Crothers 2015). A trainee entering the Fast Stream experiences different parts of the commercial process. During a series of 6- and 12-month postings across a range of departments over a period of four years, trainees are given the opportunity to experience different departmental cultures and understand commercial activity in different contexts. One posting will be in CCS. To help them acquire both a broad understanding of government and the specialist skills to become a commercial leader, trainees are also likely to complete a short secondment to the private sector and a noncommercial placement.

Trainees need or are expected to achieve at least a 2.1 rating in any subject. The selection process for Commercial Fast Stream entrants is the same as for the Finance Fast Stream (annex 2L). By the end of the scheme an individual should have the confidence to engage intelligently with those in markets, lead a procurement process, and manage contracts and stakeholder relationships. Trainees also have the opportunity to develop generalist skills, such as those required for project and change management.

Trainees also receive funding to complete the three levels of Chartered Institute of Purchasing and Supply (CIPS) diploma qualification. The combination of practical program experience and completion of CIPS examinations qualifies a trainee for CIPS membership by the end of the Fast Stream scheme. Funding for the diploma covers the costs of registering with the professional body and with the CIPS tuition provider, learning materials, tuition fees, examination fees, any exemption fees that apply, and the Institute's annual membership subscription each year. Individuals are entitled to day or block study leave.

The CCS intends to establish a central database of commercial specialists, starting with procurement professionals and extending to related professions across government. Overall the aim is to create a shared, virtual pool of expert procurement and project leaders from the Major Projects Leadership Academy (MPLA) to assist with deployment of specialist skills across departments. The government thus expects to have a higher percentage of trained, skilled, and qualified staff for the future. The Commercial Professional Skills and Competency Framework details the skills, behaviors, and competencies that civil service procurement professionals should demonstrate (Government Commercial Function [GCF] 2015a).

Procurement Professional Curriculum

Individuals are supported in their development by a baseline Procurement Professional Curriculum (GCF 2015b), which incorporates learning relevant to all procurement professionals and is available through the Civil Service e-Learning Gateway. Other professional learning and development opportunities are available through formal departmental training or informal on-the-job training, coaching, and mentoring.

A generic suite of training within the Civil Service common curriculum also supplements learning; among the elements are e-learning packages and workshops on project management, finance, commercial awareness, and negotiation skills.

Jobs are currently available to those who are already civil servants, who can apply through the Civil Service Jobs website (Civil Service n.d. b).

Other Commercial Training

Civil Service Learning offers a range of options for building core skills (Civil Service, 2015), among them

- Commercial skills for leadership courses
- Commercial Master Classes to develop or refresh skills in "planning for success," "demystifying commercial contracts," and "achieving supplier engagement"
- A one-day course in managing contractors
- Training in lean sourcing.

The CCS is also responsible for a new Commissioning Academy, designed to elevate the status of both commissioning and procurement. Effective commissioning underpins the delivery of public services. "While there are lots of examples of good practice, there is a need for capable, confident and courageous people in the public sector who are responsible for designing and delivering public services offering value for money" (Cabinet Office 2016a).

The Commissioning Academy (Cabinet Office 2016b) is a development program for senior commissioners (SCS, directors, and deputy directors) from all parts of the public sector. The program focuses on learning from examples of the most successful commissioning organizations. Individuals gain commercial skills and expertise, such as an understanding of how to influence how markets are created and shaped by government, and an ability to work collaboratively with a range of professionals to push back on legal and financial obstacles where it makes sense to do so. Managers are nominated for the academy by a senior sponsor.

Annex 2C: The Project Delivery Function

Effective delivery is particularly critical for the government's most important and high-value projects because it drives efficiencies and improves public services. The Infrastructure and Projects Authority (IPA)[8] reports jointly to the Cabinet Office and the Treasury and oversees the government's major projects portfolio, which currently consists of 200 major projects projected to cost £500bn over their lifetimes (Cabinet Office 2015b). The IPA is intended to transform the execution of government policy through world-class delivery of major projects. The IPA (in its previous form, the Major Projects Authority [MPA]) established the Major Projects Leadership Academy (MPLA) to transform the leadership of major projects. A Civil Service Project Leaders Network (CSPLN) has been established to complement and support the MPLA. The network shares project learning across government departments and meets quarterly for discussions and to consider emerging topics.

The CSPLN brings together more than 300 senior officers and project directors who lead major government projects (Cabinet Office 2015f), the government head of profession for project delivery, and other government stakeholders, such as permanent secretaries. The network offers a supportive forum of expert leaders to build the profession of project leadership within Whitehall.

In 2015–16, the IPA is launching a project delivery Fast Stream and project delivery apprenticeship recruitment streams, with the first recruits starting in 2016 (Cabinet Office 2015e). Entry is to graduates with a minimum 2.2 rating in any subject.

A new Project Leadership Programme (PLP) is also being launched in 2015–16, bringing the leadership principles established by MLPA to the 300 leaders of other government projects. While these projects may not qualify as major projects, they are nonetheless highly significant, complex, and costly and need excellent leadership. The PLP is delivered by the consortium Cranfield Management Development Ltd., which is bringing more diversity into project leadership development, complementing the MPLA. Together, the MPLA and PLP are the main development programs that support the new project delivery profession.

Project Management

There are two main training routes for project managers: the qualification from the Association of Project Management and PRINCE2 Accredited Project

Management Training (https://www.apm.org.uk). Both are short courses that do not require an entry qualification.

The Association for Project Management is committed to developing and promoting project and program management through its Five Dimensions of Professionalism. The association provides a competence framework and a progressive structure of qualifications.

The PRINCE2® project management methodology covers the management, control, and organization of a project and for full accreditation must be completed in two stages. The foundation level consists of sound development of project management methodology, working through the project lifecycle from pre-project preparation to project closure. The practitioner level builds understanding of the practical application of the methodology.

Both training routes are offered by a wide range of private providers. PRINCE2 is also available through Chartered Institute of Public Finance and Accountancy (CIPFA) as an e-learning course that requires about 65 hours. CIPFA offers a certificate in contract management; the course is Contracts and Service Level Agreements and Building Better Business Cases. The course and exam accredits individuals for the foundation stage of the Better Business Cases Program, which was developed jointly by HM Treasury and the Welsh Government and is recommended by the Treasury for those working on drafting or reviewing business cases.

Major Projects Leadership Academy

Under the Civil Service Reform Plan, all government departments agreed that by the end of 2014 "senior responsible owners" appointed to major projects must have attended the government's MPLA. The MPLA was created and is run in partnership with the Saïd Oxford Business School and Deloitte. The academy builds the skills of senior project leaders throughout government, making it easier to carry out complex projects effectively. In the future, no one will be able to lead a major government project without completing the academy program.

The executive director of the then-MPA, David Pitchford, has stated:

> What has happened here over the last 25 years, and indeed in most western jurisdictions, is that there's been a very strong trend to outsource project leadership to the consultancy sector—and that means they're also outsourcing knowledge. At the end of the project, the contractor will walk out with the money and the knowledge. (Saïd Business School n.d.)

The MPLA meets the need for major project leaders, in terms of both technical and commercial know-how and leadership capability, to return to Whitehall rather than being lost to the private sector. This ensures that the people responsible are able to lead major projects in the public sector; and it encourages agility in responding as changes in priorities, circumstances, and political direction unfold. The MPLA program is underpinned by a competency framework and curriculum.

The Role of Oxford University Saïd Business School

The MPLA program comprises three five-day residential modules delivered over a 12-month period with additional assignments interspersed. In each of the three modules experienced practitioners provide academic input and insights that blend theory with practice.

In addition to the residential courses, the school offers master classes on the role of assurance in projects. Participants are expected to apply this learning to their own work.

The Outcomes

In 2012, only a third of major projects were delivered on time and on budget; by March 2014 this had nearly doubled to two-thirds. The MPLA contributes to this improving picture by training project leaders to apply the right approaches, experience, and review processes to sustain performance over time. It gives senior responsible owners the capabilities and confidence to intervene decisively if necessary at the earliest opportunity.

Participants build an understanding of the central role of risk management in the delivery of all projects, and learn that leading a major project is not simply scaled-up project management. This reinforces the key understanding that major projects are temporary organizations in their own right and need leadership and accountability; successful major project leaders recognize engagement of stakeholders as central; and there can be incentives for core teams to remain with the project.

The achievement of all participants is assessed by a panel—the academy director, the chief executive of the IPA, and a permanent secretary—that considers participant assignments, evidence of their improved skills and capability, and their continuing professional development. Through the MPLA, annually over 100 leaders of major projects throughout government are able to build their competence and capabilities.

Annex 2D: Chartered Finance and Accountancy Institutes

There are four main professional accountancy and finance institutes in England and Wales[9] that train people working in the public sector for a full professional qualification:

- **Chartered Association of Certified Accountants (ACCA):** The Association of Chartered Certified Accountants (http://www.accaglobal.com/U.K.) has 162,000 members and 428,000 students in 173 countries. It offers business-relevant, first-choice qualifications to people of application, ability, and ambition around the world who seek a rewarding career in accountancy, finance, and management.
- **Chartered Institute of Management Accountants (CIMA):** The CIMA (http://www.cimaglobal.com) has more than 229,000 members and students in 176 countries. Its goal is to establish management accounting as the most

valued profession in business worldwide. It teaches skills for strategic advice, managing risk, and making decisions. The CIMA syllabus is designed to deliver a thorough understanding of all aspects of business so members can contribute in many areas of an organization. CIMA aims to qualify members to work anywhere in an organization, not just in finance.

- **Chartered Institute of Public Finance and Accountancy (CIPFA):** The CIPFA (https://www.cipfa.org.uk) has 14,000 members and an evolving global reach for trainees from as wide a geographic range as Slovenia, Lesotho, and Bangladesh. CIPFA is the only professional accountancy body in the world that is exclusively dedicated to public finance. CIPFA's portfolio of qualifications lays the foundation for a career in public finance. It offers the benchmark professional qualification for public sector accountants, a postgraduate diploma for people already working in leadership positions, a new diploma in International Public Sector Accounting Standards (IPSAS), and a new finance business partnering qualification. They are taught in-house at the CIPFA Education and Training Centre and other places of learning around the world. CIPFA works with governments, accountancy entities, donors, the wider development community, and others to improve public financial management (PFM) globally.

- **Institute of Chartered Accountants in England and Wales (ICAEW):** ICEAW (http://www.icaew.com) has a membership of over 144,000 chartered accountants around the world. Its aims are to provide qualifications and professional development; share knowledge, insight, and technical expertise; promote, develop, and support members; and protect the quality and integrity of the profession. The ICAEW recently launched a new IPSAS certificate that can be earned via e-learning.

The professional qualification syllabi offered by these institutes share some common elements, though each has elements that are unique. In addition to their core professional qualification for students who work in finance, they offer a number of subsidiary and complementary short-course qualifications.

The institutes also contribute to the development of professional accounting and audit standards, either directly, as in the case of CIPFA with respect to public sector standards, or indirectly by active commentary in consultations on new standards or regulations issued by regulators like the Financial Reporting Council and the Auditing Practice Board. All the institutes consult with government on development of the government finance function.

CIPFA is the only institute dedicated to the public sector; it carries out research on central and local government, the health sector, charities, and other public bodies and entities. The research and publications of the other institutes have traditionally been focused on the needs of the private sector, though many elements of their good practice findings apply to the public sector. Association of Chartered Certified Accountants (ACCA), Chartered Institute of Management Accountants (CIMA), and ICAEW produce publications for the public sector, and ACCA and CIMA often make them available on their websites to both members and nonmembers. Some publications on the ICAEW website that deal with the public sector are only accessible to members, although nonmembers may access a number of documents covering the central government.

Entry Qualifications

All the institutes offer an entry route for school leavers. In partnership with the Association of Accounting Technicians (annex 2E), they all offer talented individuals the opportunity to qualify as an accounting technician and a professional qualification in as little as four years by joining the Association of Accounting Technicians (AAT) at the highest level, 4. Trainees in the government's Fast Track apprenticeship scheme follow this route to professional qualifications.

Graduates with a degree in any subject can take a direct entry route to professional institute qualifications, a route that normally takes three years. Although not necessarily required by the institute, the government sets minimum standards of academic achievement for degree holders for entry to the training program with any institute. For some qualifications, such as Institute of Chartered Accountants in England and Wales (ICAEW), most employers prefer that students also have a minimum Universities and Colleges Admissions Service tariff score of 280 or above (or international equivalent), covering both school AS and A2 levels. However, the ACCA entry requirement is more liberal.

All the institutes offer some exemption from one or more examination elements if the student has either earned a degree in accounting or finance or a significant part of their degree work covered relevant subjects. Some of the institutes support degrees at universities, as ACCA does at Oxford Brookes University, that are designed to offer maximum exemptions from their qualification requirements; all students must take examinations to earn professional qualifications.

Exemption is not guaranteed. Experience suggests that students taking a related degree do not necessarily fare any better than those who have taken, for example, Greek (in 2013, 50 percent of ICAEW students had non-business-related degrees in subjects like psychology, music, and languages).

Qualification Structures

For all the qualifications, students must take formal examinations and obtain a range of work experience while studying. The work experience must be recorded and verified by an employer signature. CIMA, ICAEW, and CIPFA require examinations in all subjects unless an exemption has been granted; ACCA offers a limited number of optional subjects.

Although the various qualifications cover some common subjects, such as corporate reporting, financial management, audit, and assurance, the exact content of the qualifications differs slightly. All the institutes review their qualification requirements regularly as needs evolve.

CIMA structures its qualification as a three-layered route through management from the base up to the strategic level, with learning tailored to the knowledge that would be required at each level. ACCA, CIPFA, and ICAEW recognize a professional level of knowledge and an application of that knowledge in advanced management papers.

ACCA, CIMA, and CIPFA all explicitly recognize the need for a professional examination in governance, risk, and ethics. All the institutes have partnerships with a college or university to offer a sponsored degree, such as the ACCA-sponsored BSc Applied in accounting and finance at Oxford Brookes and the ICAEW Undergraduate Partnership Programme with Manchester, Warwick, and Cardiff Universities.

Accreditation of Employers

Where individuals train with an institute through an employer, the institute assesses the support available to the student during the training period. This includes a commitment from the employer that the student will be given access to the range of work experience required to meet the demands of the qualification; that the employer will record the experience and review it with the student; and that there will be support for the student to pursue continuous professional development after successfully completing the qualification.

Accreditation and Approval of Training Providers

Most training providers are private companies, of which there are many. A few universities and some colleges also train students for the professional qualifications. All the institutes carry out some assessment of at least a core of training providers (for example, 54 providers in the U.K. are classified as "quality" providers offering training in the full CIMA professional qualification). The assessment typically looks at capacity to provide training (for example, numbers of trainers and their qualifications), facilities for classroom teaching (if required), quality of the materials provided to the students, records of student attendance (if applicable), and records of student feedback provided to students and employers. The assessment is followed up at intervals by unannounced institute visits to confirm that providers still meet the agreed standards. All the institutes remove providers who do not meet the standards.

CIPFA prefers to focus on a small group of training providers, such as Kaplan (http://www.kaplan.co.U.K.) and Nottingham Business School, as well as providing training directly in a dedicated training center.

All training providers offer a range of teaching methods from classroom learning through training on-line. All the institutes list accredited training providers on their websites, although the list may not be exhaustive for a particular qualification.

Annex 2E: AAT: Association of Accounting Technicians[10]

The AAT has 125,000 members in 90 countries and saw a 2.6 percent increase in new student registrations in 2014. With a goal of putting AAT at the heart of every business, its suite of qualifications is designed to inculcate the practical skills needed in the workplace.

AAT provides a number of programs that either lead to qualifications in their own right or form the foundation of a professional qualification pursued through one of the finance and accountancy institutes. The AAT Accounting Qualification opens entry into a career in accounting and finance without expensive university fees.[11] The qualification is made up of three levels: introductory level 2 certificate, intermediate diploma in accounting, and level 4 diploma for students who have progressed through the first two levels or are at a more advanced stage in their career. The level 4 diploma is the direct entry point for school leavers who have been accepted for the government Fast Track apprenticeship scheme; usually they have good school-leaving qualifications.

At each level there are examinations, and most of the examinations are mandatory. The final level provides optional specialist subjects. AAT also provides shorter, complementary qualifications, such as a certificate in bookkeeping and an award in computerized accounting.

Upon successful completion of the main AAT qualification, a student can continue studies with another chartered accountancy entity. All U.K. chartered and certified accountancy entities recognize the AAT Accounting Qualification, and AAT students can receive exemptions from certain modules. In general, the AAT fast-track route allows nongraduates to achieve chartered status more quickly than the university path. AAT is sponsored by all the professional accounting bodies.

AAT has over 500 training providers in the U.K. and across the world. Training can be classroom or distance learning or on-line learning. AAT also offers a range of continuing education courses (CPD Pack https://www.aat.org.uk/sites/default/files/assets/2014-cpd-programme.pdf), webinars, and other events for members. The AAT CPD policy came into force in January 2014. It complies with the standards of the International Federation of Accountants, of which AAT was elected a full member in 2013.

Annex 2F: CIIA: The Chartered Institute of Internal Auditors

The CIIA has about 8,500 members across the U.K. and Ireland, of which some 2,160 are in the public sector, though CIIA does not distinguish how many members come from which part of the public sector. CIIA is an affiliate of the global Institute of Internal Audit (IIA), which has 180,000 members in 190 countries. Internal auditors in the U.K. and Ireland must be CIIA members in good standing to study for an IIA global certification. Membership must be maintained in order to use the designation.

The CIIA is the only professional association for internal auditors in the U.K. and Ireland. Its goals are to

- develop the profession to ensure that it has the knowledge, skills, and expertise to be essential to the success of organizations, and
- promote the role and value of the profession to ensure that it is recognized as essential to success.

There are two main ways to join CIIA, as a student member or as an affiliate:

1. Student membership is for internal auditors who want to study for professional qualifications in internal auditing, starting with the new Chartered Internal Auditor (CIA) program, previously the IIA Diploma. Student membership can last up to four years, the length of the study period.
2. Affiliate membership is open to anyone working in internal audit who does not wish to take a professional qualification. Individuals wishing to take CIIA modular training, such as the IIA Certificate, should also join as an affiliate member or apply to be chartered by experience (see next section).

CIIA Qualifications

The first-level qualification is the new Certified Internal Auditor (CIA, which requires a time commitment of 60–80 hours each for CIA parts 1 and 2, and 140–160 hours for CIA part 3 (https://www.iia.org.uk/qualifications/certified-internal-auditor/). There are three exams for part 3. The student has four years to complete the CIA program, which includes the time to meet the experience requirement. Applicants must either hold a degree; have 2 years of post-secondary education and 2 years of internal audit experience; or have 4 years of internal audit experience. Before being awarded the certificate the student must have experience of working in an internal audit or related role.

The second-level qualification is the CIA, for which students must pass three case study exams to test both technical knowledge and leadership ability or must demonstrate their competence via the institute "chartered by experience route." Most individuals take the examination.

The three case study exams cover internal audit, organizational, and ethical leadership. The student is presented with the case study immediately before the exam, which is computer-based. Students must also complete a professional experience journal, covering about three years of working as an internal auditor providing independent assurance to an organization on risks and controls.

Individuals wishing to take the CIA case study exams must be CIA-qualified (or have passed the exams, even if not yet completing the other requirements), or hold the Institute of Internal Auditor Diploma.

The Open University has endorsed the IIA qualifications and awarded them credits (https://www.iia.org.uk/openuniversity). For qualifying as a CIA, the Open University awards 120 credits toward a master's degree. CIIA Learning is the CIIA's in-house provider of programs; other accredited providers include Birmingham City Business School (https://www.bcu.ac.uk/business-school/services-for-business/management-leadership-development/ciagrm/professional-courses), for the IIA diploma) and Birmingham City University Business School (BHBi) Consultancy Ltd, a private consultancy (https://www.bhbi.co.uk).

The CIIA also carries out research on public sector topics. For example, it works with CIPFA to improve internal audit in government and across the public sector; working with internal audit standard setters, this collaboration has resulted in the U.K.'s first set of public sector internal audit standards.

At the instigation of the Treasury and other standard setters, the Internal Audit Standards Advisory Board was established to draft standards for the whole U.K. public sector, based on the IIA Global International Standards.

Annex 2G: CIPS: The Chartered Institute of Purchasing and Supply[12]

The CIPS, which has 115,000 members worldwide, is the largest professional body representing procurement and supply chain professionals. CIPS exists to promote and develop high standards of professional skill, ability, and integrity in all those engaged in purchasing and supply chain management. CIPS supports individuals, organizations, and the profession as a whole.

The CIPS curriculum provides the baseline learning relevant to all procurement specialists within central government. The Civil Service procurement profession is working with CIPS to tailor a curriculum for it and the commercial profession; training is available through the Civil Service Learning Gateway. This curriculum underpins the procurement profession competency framework, which sets out the skills, behaviors, and competencies that civil service procurement professionals should demonstrate. The Joint Procurement and Commercial Curriculum provides other professional learning and development opportunities through the formal training arrangements of each profession or through informal on-the-job training (OJT), coaching, and mentoring. (The Commercial-Professional Curriculum is available at https://www.gov.uk/government/uploads/system/uploads/attachment_data/file/418424/Commercial-Professional-Curriculum-Revised_23_03_15.pdf.)

The Skills Level

The CIPS curriculum is aligned to the three levels of expertise required for the skills elements of any role that an individual is expected to perform:

Awareness/Developing: "Awareness" demonstrates that an individual is able to understand major issues and their implications. Civil servants may be early in their procurement career or the subject may not be a priority skill within their current role. "Developing" demonstrates behaviors and outcomes that are above awareness but that the staff member has not had sufficient opportunity or experience to put into practice to achieve the practitioner level.

Practitioner: Based on significant commercial experience and qualifications, an individual displays detailed knowledge of the subject and is capable not only of undertaking procurement functions but also of providing guidance and advice to others.

Expert: Individuals have extensive experience and applied knowledge of the subject. They have significant commercial experience and may be at the top of their profession in terms of skills.

CIPS offers five qualifications to support professional development in procurement and supply. On successful completion of the diploma and the advanced and professional diplomas and in conjunction with three years' experience of responsibility in procurement and supply, students may apply for full membership in CIPS.

Entry Requirements

There are three possible starting points for CIPS qualifications:

- Certificate in procurement and supply operations
- Advanced certificate in procurement and supply operations
- Diploma in procurement and supply.

The first two are building-block qualifications designed for people who are new to the profession or who do not meet the minimum entry requirements for the diploma qualification. Students seeking to start at diploma level need at least two A-levels (or international equivalent), a CIPS advanced certificate qualification, or two years' experience in a business environment.

Registered CIPS students holding certain qualifications or degrees may apply for exemptions. It is possible to apply for exemptions unit-by-unit for all qualifications from the Certificate in Procurement and Supply Operations through to the Professional Diploma in Procurement and Supply. A student can only apply for exemptions from a maximum of three units per qualification level; the student must take a minimum of two CIPS assessments per qualification level. A detailed guide to the core units of the curriculum and how to apply for exemptions is available at http://www.cips.org.

Each unit studied is supported by a detailed learning outcomes mapping document to demonstrate learning and the hours of study a student needs to complete. The program supports a range of study modes, among them modular intensive study sessions, often at weekends; blended sessions of structured classroom learning and e-learning or on-line tutor support; distance learning with some support from a tutor on-line; self-study using CIPS learning material and website resources; and 250 hours of e-learning at the student's own computer.

The CIPS provides all these options through its own network (https://www.cips.org/cips-for-business/people-development/corporate-academy). There is also a network of about 75 approved study centers in the U.K. CIPS works closely with the network to make sure the centers can meet the standards it has defined in terms of quality of staff, facilities, resources, and customer care. Centers are asked to complete an annual report, a self-assessment of their performance over the past year, and a statement of how the assessment has helped the center improve. CIPS looks at examination and assessment results and reviews feedback from students. CIPS also visits U.K. study centers annually to assess suitability for continued approval and for upgrading to a higher category. The institute takes action when any concerns arise, and in serious cases it may withdraw approval.

CIPS also accredits a number of university degrees, such as the MBA in strategy and procurement management at the University of Birmingham.

Accredited worldwide: CIPS qualifications are designed to meet the highest standards to ensure that the profession can claim consistently high workforce competence. The CIPS Awarding Body is regulated by Ofqual, the official examination regulator, in England and Northern Ireland; CIPS qualifications are recognized either on the Qualifications and Credit Framework or the National Qualifications Framework. CIPS is also regulated by the Welsh Government.

Assessment

All the units in CIPS qualifications are assessed by an examination, although some also have an alternative nonexamined option.

Being a member of the institute provides a range of other benefits in terms of professional development, such as a comprehensive online resource covering such procurement topics as LEAN and continuous improvement. The institute arranges a variety of continuing professional development (CPD) courses on topics like effective negotiation, the legal aspects of purchasing and events management. These are provided through e-learning and formal workshops.

Annex 2H: Examples of Specialist Public Financial Management (PFM) Areas

Treasury Function: Although the Debt Management Office is likely to be the single biggest user of this specialty and there are Treasury functions in certain other departments, such as the Ministry of Defence, this role is more common in local government. The main qualification provider for this is the Association of Corporate Treasurers, though Kaplan and CIPFA, among others, offer short specialist courses.

Risk and Compliance Function: Most internal and external auditors have training in risk management and can train employees in an organization to the extent required in most circumstances. All departments have a senior manager for risk and compliance who reports to the board, and this person is likely to have a specific risk management qualification and significant experience in an industry where risk is a particular issue, such as insurance. The main qualification is issued by the Institute of Risk Management (IRM), though there are other qualifications within the insurance and health and safety sectors.

Fraud/Counterfraud: This is a potential growth area; the current government is actively investing to address the problem. Fraud is a specialist subject. Entry to the specialty is difficult without significant prior experience either with the police or as an auditor who has been involved in a fraud investigation.

Treasury Function

There is no formal training route into the Treasury function for civil servants as there is for Procurement, Finance, or Audit. Civil servants carrying out a Treasury function may hold a specialist Treasury Management qualification from an entity like the Association of Corporate Treasurers; a finance and accountancy qualification; completion of a specific course through an institute like CIPFA; or perhaps a qualification from a previous job either in local government (for example, through the Association of District or County Treasurers) or from a private organization such as a bank. Alternatively, experienced senior financial managers with a qualification in Treasury management may be recruited for a specific position, for example, in the Debt Management Office.

Treasury management incorporates such elements as risk management, cash and liquidity management, regulation and law, business and operational risk, and foreign currency management. The Association of Corporate Treasurers provides a range of certificates and diplomas building to full membership status.

Risk and Compliance Function

This description focuses on the risk element of the function. There is a short introduction to risk on the Civil Service E-Learning Gateway, which all civil servants are encouraged to read to gain an understanding of risk. Internal Audit may also run short workshops to support the e-learning and further embed the concepts of risk throughout the organization.

The IRM International Diploma in Risk Management is equivalent to a post-graduate degree (https://www.theirm.org/training/all-courses). It is a key qualification for anyone pursuing a career in risk management and is relevant to all sectors, organizations, and countries. The diploma verifies that the holder has the knowledge and practical skills to formulate and execute successful risk management strategies.

Those trained by IRM come from a very diverse range of risk management backgrounds; this qualification is suitable for those specializing in risk at very senior levels within departments. It gives members an online resource center for further learning, such as risk management standards and guides offering practical insights into and tools for the main risk management topics.

Fraud and Counter-fraud

"At least 2 per cent of the government's benefits expenditure has been taken up by fraud and error since 2005" (https://www.civilserviceworld.com/fraud-and-error-now-2-of-welfare). Tackling fraud and error offers a real opportunity for reducing waste of funds. The government has announced that it would save £2.3 billion by strengthening "Whitehall's capacity to prevent error and tackle fraud in the benefit and tax credit systems" by the end of 2014–15. There are two main options for training in counter-fraud.

University of Portsmouth Fraud Courses: The Counter Fraud Professional Accreditation Board (CFPAB) includes representatives of government departments, CIPFA, and the National Fraud Authority. The CFPAB (http://www.port.

ac.uk/institute-of-criminal-justice-studies/counter-fraud-professional-accredita-tion-board) sets and maintains professional standards in the delivery of a portfo-lio of professional training courses in counter-fraud work, encompassing a foun-dation level syllabus and qualification. It also formally recognizes successful completion of the portfolio.

The CFPAB oversees the quality and effectiveness of counter-fraud courses and promotes such training. It offers a number of awards from counter-fraud technician through to graduate counter-fraud specialist. Government depart-ments that are represented on the CFPAB Board, such as the DWP and HM Revenue and Customs, may also train their own staff but do not generally offer this training commercially.

Accredited Counter Fraud Specialist: Foundation-level Training: This is a university-accredited professional qualification designed by specialist counter-fraud practitioners to reflect operational needs and set a common standard for core skills and knowledge. There are four modules that must be completed in order and that take students through a complete fraud investigation. The four week-long modules use a realistic case scenario to explore the principles, skills, procedures, and techniques required of an effective counter-fraud specialist and the related legislation. It is a pass/fail course that uses a variety of assessments to cover different learning styles, with delegates given an opportunity to discuss the progress of the case file with a trainer at the end of each week. The pass floor for each assessment is 70 percent.

Annex 2I: Civil Service Talent Toolkit (https://civilservicelearning. civilservice.gov.uk/sites/default/files/corporate_talent_strategy_v0f. pdf)

The toolkit contains four modules for talent management.

1. The "9 box grid" maps an individual's potential and performance, in the pro-cess helping build the talent profile for the population under consideration. The toolkit is applied to all SCS 1 staff; grades G6 and G7 are assessed at least annually, though other staff groups can also be assessed.
2. The Critical Roles Succession Plan identifies future candidates for defined roles or groups of roles and highlights where the coverage is not deep enough. It helps to assess the strength of the talent pipeline and also what is needed to build the readiness of individuals for succession. At the basic level, critical roles should be identified at the most senior levels of the organization because these positions are, as a general rule, likely to cause the greatest disruption if unfilled for a long period. A combination of the 9 box grid and critical roles succession planning can make it clearer whether the right people are in the right roles at the right time.
3. A leadership team overview provides a snapshot of team potential, expertise, and stability to measure the health of the team mix and to identify any action needed.

Figure A2I.1 Use of the 9 Box Grid

Potential
(Column here is ascending scale from 3. to 1.)

	Shows Early Promise (4+ years)	*Has High Potential (1–3 years)*	*Star Performer (ready now)*
1. Likely to progress beyond current grade	High potential with strong initial impact, but new or inexperienced in current role. *This is a transition marking: Individuals in this box would be expected to move across or down the grid within 18 months.*	Frequently achieves challenging and stretch goals with strong demonstration of potential. Performance continually improving, adaptable to change, and acknowledged as a leader.	An exceptional performer who stands out from peers. Has Realized potential, ready for/will be successful at next level now. Acknowledged as a skilled leader and role model.
	Future Achiever	*Solid Contributor*	*Strong Performer*
2. Could progress beyond current grade	Either new to post, demonstrating ability but too early to form judgment, or gap in performance compared with expectations. *This is a transition marking: Individuals are not expected to remain in this box for more than 12 months.*	Valued at this level and in this role. Performance is good, achieving normal high expectations, and has the potential to keep developing and to deliver more in either scale or complexity.	A consistently strong performer, delivering excellent value. Exhibits some behaviors and competencies beyond current level but not all.
	Incomplete Performer	*Satisfactory Contributor*	*Good Performer*
3. Best suited to current grade	Performance is inconsistent or not fully effective. Has competency gaps or behavioral style issues.	*Meets performance expectations at this level. Has realized professional and leadership capability.* *There is an expectation that individuals in this box for more than 2 years will be subject to further review.*	Highly valued at this level & in current role. A consistent strong performer who is a core team member.
	Inconsistent or Incomplete Performer	Fully Effective	Exceptional Performer
	Performance (ascending) ⟶		

Source: Civil Service Human Resources.

4. Vacancy Maps provide a picture of current and planned vacancies to identify potential internal candidates and to help decide on the approach to filling the vacancy.

Annex 2J: Civil Service Local: Cross-Government Mentoring

Civil Service Local (https://www.gov.uk/government/groups/civil-service-local)
is a cross-government initiative actively promoting and delivering greater collaborative working and reform at a local level. The mentoring scheme (https://
civilservicelocal.blog.gov.uk/tag/mentoring) is a Civil Service Local initiative to
help deliver key elements of the Civil Service Reform Plan, complementing the
role of Civil Service Learning. It is a low-cost workplace learning and development opportunity that will build the capability of staff by strengthening skills
and deploying talent.

In essence, mentoring recognizes the value of learning from each other. Having
a workplace mentor outside of the line management structure with experience in
one or more areas helps the mentee achieve his or her full potential. Also, since
mentoring is a mutual relationship, there are opportunities to exchange knowledge, share good practices, and learn from one another. For both parties mentoring
is a relatively long-term one-to-one relationship and a personal development
opportunity.

The local scheme operates to attract both civil servants interested in being a
mentor and those who would like to have a mentor. Mentor applications are
welcomed from people who have received mentoring training or have mentoring
experience. Mentee applications are welcome from all staff, though they have to
have the support of their line managers and to have discussed how this fits into
their learning and development plan. (The coordinator sometimes has to work to
balance mentors and mentee needs. For instance, the North East may have 37
mentors and 33 mentees, but more mentors are needed.)

Mentoring can take place at the workplace of the mentee or the mentor or
another location convenient for both. Together they decide the format of the
sessions; they do not all need to be face-to-face; both may want to keep in touch
between sessions through e-mail, phone or video conferencing, or text. The
mentoring scheme has no direct costs, but there may be some travel costs
incurred to enable mentee and mentor to meet. The employer will cover reasonable costs.

Initially the mentoring arrangement is likely to last 12 months, although the
actual time depends on the objectives and goals identified by the mentee.

The mentor is usually at least a grade above the mentee and within a reasonable travelling distance. The scheme coordinator for a region looks for a mentor
with the expertise the mentee is looking for and then asks if that mentor is willing to be contacted by the prospective mentee. If the answer is yes, the coordinator asks the mentee to contact the mentor; both parties need to agree that they
are a suitable match and they may decide on this over the phone or at an infor-

mal meeting. Once they have established that they are a match, they let the coordinator know when they plan to meet formally for the first time. So that the organizers can evaluate the scheme, the mentee completes an initial bench-mark form and mentor and mentee will receive evaluation forms at 3, 6, and 12 months and when the relationship is ended.

Annex 2K: Graduate Entry to the Civil Service Fast Stream[13]

For 2015–16 the Fast Stream encompassed entry into the PFM disciplines of Finance, Internal Audit, and Commercial. The selection process is designed to identify those who have the potential to benefit from the program and become the leaders of tomorrow.

All candidates are invited to complete numerical and verbal reasoning tests only. If candidates pass these successfully, their eligibility to apply for the Fast Stream will be checked and their responses to the competencies section of the application evaluated. Those who pass at this stage will be invited to a one-day assessment, where they will first be required to complete an online personality potential profile questionnaire before attending the assessment center itself (see figure A2K.1).

Candidates take tests at two points. The first is the verbal and numerical reasoning tests on-line, which are self-assessed. The verbal test has 40 questions (20 minutes allowed), and numeric tests have 18 questions (22 minutes).

These tests are exactly the same as the on-line selection tests the candidate will later have to pass to be shortlisted for the E-tray exercise (see below).

The online tests are used to decide whether the candidate is suitable for the Fast Stream. In addition to the verbal and numeric tests there is also a Fast Stream Competency multiple choice questionnaire (not timed but taking about 35 minutes). The competency questionnaire tests behaviors that relate to the competencies the Civil Service looks for in Fast Streamers.

All candidates who are invited to the Fast Stream Assessment Center are re-tested; if there is a significant discrepancy between the score achieved at this stage and the candidate's online test scores, the application will be reviewed. Personal integrity is considered absolutely essential in the Civil Service; any form of misrepresentation during the selection process results in the candidate's elimination from the competition.

Candidates for whom there are no discrepancies are admitted to the E-tray exercise. This tests a candidate's ability to handle a workload that is typical of the requests and tasks that arrive in the email inbox of a Fast Streamer. The test, which takes about two and a half hours, can be completed on a home computer. The timed exercise has three parts:

1. Reading and comprehending background material
2. Identifying from a choice of options the most and least appropriate responses to a series of e-mails

Figure A2K.1 Steps in the Civil Service Fast Stream Process

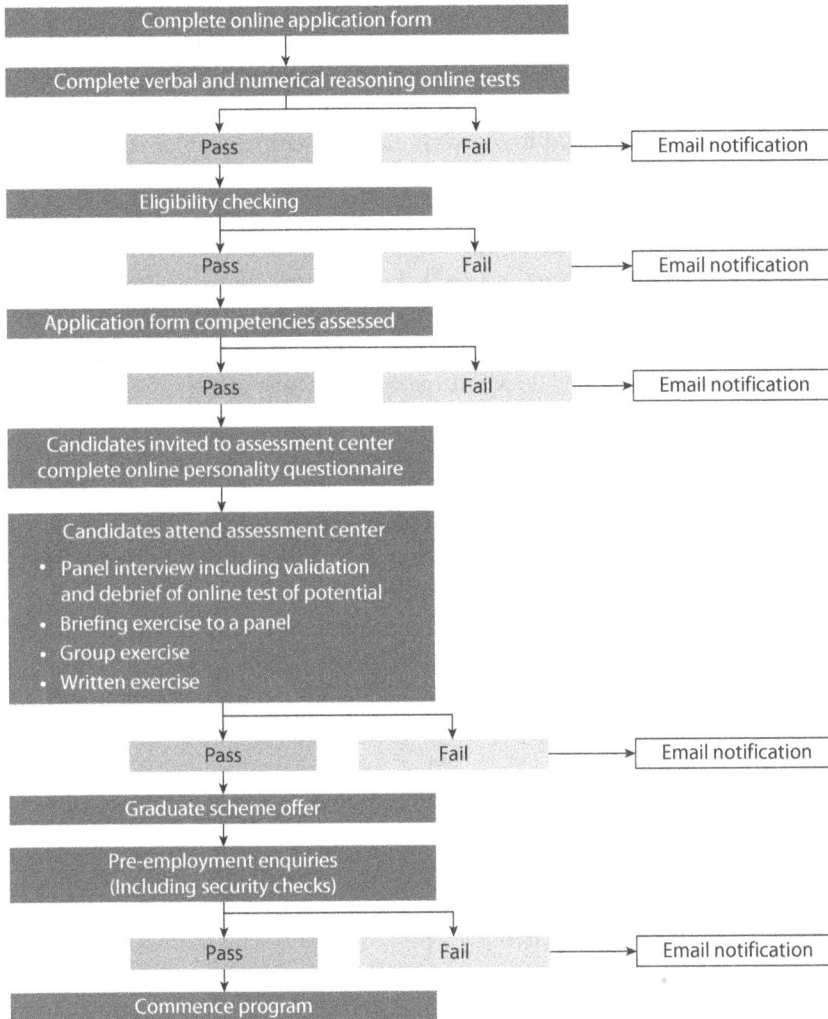

Source: Civil Service Fast Stream: How to Apply 2014.

3. Writing a response to a request for information, using what the candidate has learned during the earlier stages.

The final element in the process is attendance at the one-day assessment center in London.

Fast Streamers can come from any background, with any kind of degree, although for 2015–16 many streams required a minimum degree achievement. However, there are some qualities that potential Fast Streamers must have:

Setting direction: The candidate must be innovative, always looking for opportunities to improve what the Civil Service does and working in smarter, more focused ways. The candidate must show clarity of thought, using sound judgment, evidence, and knowledge to provide accurate, informed, and professional advice.

Engaging people: Fast Streamers will lead from the front, communicating with clarity, conviction, and enthusiasm. To do this they need to focus on continuous learning for themselves, others, and the organization. This will help them create and maintain positive, professional, and trusted working relationships with a wide range of people to get things done. Underpinning all this are principles of fairness for all and a dedication to a diverse range of citizens.

Delivering results: This includes applying program and project management approaches, working to agreed goals and activities, and dealing with challenges in a responsive and constructive way. They will also need a commercial, financial, and sustainable mind-set to ensure that everything they do adds value and works to stimulate economic growth. They need to demonstrate an understanding of efficiency, effectiveness, and economy in the delivery of public services.

There is no age limit and it does not matter how long ago the person graduated (though it is expected that they will serve for several years before retirement). What is vital are skills, attitude, and outlook.

- Starting salaries are between £25,000 and £27,000.
- Pay increases are based purely on performance. On promotion (currently on average after four to five years) candidates may earn over £45,000.
- Fast Streamers are given a permanent employment contract from the start, provided they meet performance and development standards.
- Benefits are flexible working hours, Civil Service pension scheme, and 22 days' annual holiday on entry plus 9 public and additional holidays.

This is a leadership development program; graduates are given responsibility quickly. Individuals are inducted into both the Fast Stream and the Civil Service to set the career in context.

There is a dedicated Civil Service learning and development pathway in partnership with Civil Service Resourcing for Fast Streamers. The training and development package includes

- A combination of formal training courses and on-the-job learning
- Regular feedback and performance reviews to inform personal development
- A mentor or another Fast Streamer to support an individual's development
- Time spent at learning events, e-learning, volunteering, job-shadowing, and more
- The chance for supported study to earn a range of professional qualifications (postgraduate certificates, CIPD, Chartered Institute of Management Accountants [CIMA], and others).

At the end of the program Fast Streamers will have acquired skills and knowledge in a wide range of important areas, among them people management, commercial awareness, financial management, project and program management, change management, and digital delivery.

Fast Streamers are also encouraged to take time out before joining the Civil Service, by becoming a teacher or a social entrepreneur, or work with a children's charity to widen their experience and become more rounded individuals.

Notes

1. John Manzoni was appointed Chief Executive of the Civil Service in October 2014 to lead the development of the "functional leadership model." This model has a head of each profession determining the operating model for the function, recruiting and deploying staff across government, and setting common standards for departments.

2. An arm's-length body is an organization that delivers a public service, is not a ministerial government department, and operates to a greater or lesser extent at a distance from Ministers. The term can include non departmental public bodies (NDPBs), executive agencies, non-ministerial departments, public corporations, NHS bodies, and inspectorates. Such bodies are considered accountable to Parliament.

3. This report focuses on central government in England and Wales—in addition there are two more institutes in the United Kingdom: Institute of Chartered Accountants of Scotland (ICAS) in Scotland (www.icas.com) and ICAI in Northern Ireland (http://ulster.charteredaccountants.ie/).

4. Some institutes offer alternative routes to qualification for individuals who do not meet these necessary minimum requirements. For example, Institute of Chartered Accountants in England and Wales (ICAEW) offers a Certificate in Finance, Accounting and Business, which is the first six papers of the Association of Chartered Accountants (ACA) qualification. ICAEW reports that in its experience more employers are accepting entrants who are not graduates.

5. Classroom training is traditional face-to-face tuition; e-learning is conducted via pre-recorded electronic media, typically on the Internet, though sometimes through media packages stored on the student's local work computers; online learning typically employs a tutor at a remote location conducting an interactive live learning session to a class of students connected via their local computers; distance learning offers students an opportunity to study from home at their own pace and in their own time using a mix of media (books, Internet etc.)

6. http://www.accaglobal.com/uk/en/student/getting-started/exemptions.html.

7. Data visualization: presentation of data in a pictorial, chart/graphical format; decision makers are able to see data and analysis visually, which helps them grasp difficult concepts or identify new patterns. This area is considered an important new form of communication for those managing complex data profiles.

8. Tony Meggs was appointed interim Head of the Major Projects Authority (MPA) in July 2015 as a senior executive, having significant experience as a functional leader in the private sector leading collaborations with several businesses and universities. Meggs set up the BP project leadership programme (PLP) that was the inspiration for the Major Projects Leadership Academy (MPLA). He also co-chaired a major study at Massachusetts Institute of Technology. In November 2015 the government announced the merger of the MPA with Infrastructure U.K.; the new organization is called Infrastructure and Projects Authority (IPA). The new organization will report to the Chancellor of the Exchequer and the Minister for the Cabinet Office (Cabinet Office 2015d).

9. This report focuses on central government England and Wales—there are two other institutes operating in the United Kingdom: ICAS in Scotland (https://www.icas.com) and ICAI in Northern Ireland (http://ulster.charteredaccountants.ie/).

10. https://www.aat.org.uk

11. An average university degree will cost £27,000 (2013–14); gaining the Association of Accounting Technicians (AAT) qualification will cost about £500, and the government will provide tuition fees, materials and paid work experience along with training.

12. http://www.cips.org/en-GB/membership

13. Cabinet Office n.d.

CHAPTER 3

Supporting Human Resource Management Processes

Structure of Jobs

Public financial management (PFM) roles can be grouped as follows:

1. Three core functions within Finance: decision support, operational finance, and reporting and control (annexes 3A and 3B). Each has job descriptions that define responsibilities and the required personal knowledge, skills, and experience
2. Internal audit (external audit is independent of the Civil Service)
3. Commercial services (corporate finance, procurement, supply chain, contract management)
4. Risk management (often a specialist role at a senior level)
5. Asset management

Corporate centers of excellence for each professional function help give a government-wide perspective: the government finance function in the Treasury; the Government Internal Audit Agency (GIAA 2015) led by the head of government internal audit); and in the Cabinet Office the Crown Commercial Services (CCS) Group (commercial profession) and the Major Projects Leadership Academy (MPLA) (project delivery profession). Central heads of professions draft and oversee the execution of strategies for improving the management of financial resources across central government, and they oversee the selection, recruitment, deployment, career, and continuing professional development of trainees and finance professionals. Department heads of profession present their bids for new graduates through the central recruitment scheme to the central head of profession, who then asks Civil Service Human Resources (HR) to manage recruitment of those graduates; the departments are charged for the service provided.

Grading and Pay

Two features of the way civil servants are paid are distinctive:

- Pay is not centrally determined. Except for the SCS cadre, Civil Service organizations are responsible for their own arrangements for pay, grading, and performance management arrangements for staff.
- Performance-related pay is also delegated to departments, though this element of the pay package is quite small.

Departments have some flexibility, as long as their budget for salaries and wages fits within the specified remit for that year. Departments do have to apply the Civil Service Pay Guidance for the budget year (HM Treasury 2015b) in determining pay levels and to retain a recognizable government-wide grading and pay structure. Thus they do not have total flexibility, though some believe that they should (Brecknell 2014).

One of the outcomes of the delegated-pay approach is that trainees from different parts of the Civil Service start their careers with different benefit packages. The starting salary for graduates entering the Finance Fast Stream for 2015–16 ranges from £25,000 to £27,000 a year (Civil Service n.d. b.). This compares with the median of £28,000 for graduates of any discipline entering accountancy or professional service firms in 2014–15, and is slightly lower than for new engineering or medicine graduates (Complete University Guide 2016).

Professional qualifications that relate to the job may attract an annual allowance, although this varies by department (see annex 3C for examples of trainee progression allowances). Once individuals achieve the PFM qualification, if they remain in a designated PFM role, they retain the allowance. Specialist pay may be provided to people with qualifications that are in high demand.

If students from the same employer, the Civil Service, train as one group and then receive different allowances for their qualification (and ultimately different first-year salaries) according to the policies of their department, disquiet and demotivation may result. This would not happen in the private sector; students from one employer normally all receive the same pay rewards for training.

The delegated pay approach is intended to allow departments to reflect market rates, to an extent. While this is of some benefit to the grades up to the SCS, at the higher levels the disparity between public and private salaries is significant. The main difficulty in making comparisons is that it is very difficult to find jobs that are really comparable—one reason why the Office of National Statistics does not produce the data.

Recruitment and Selection

The statutory basis for management of the Civil Service is set out in the Constitutional Reform and Governance Act of 2010. It makes the Civil Service Commission (2015) responsible for ensuring that selection is on merit after fair and open competition. The Commission's 2015 Recruitment Principles outline the basis for exceptions to, and responsibilities of departments for, meeting the requirement. These principles give departments and agencies freedom to decide on how they will approach recruitment, provided the approach is consistent with the principles. Departments and agencies must manage staff in a way that complies with both the Recruitment Principles and employment law.

While management of HR policies for the Civil Service is the responsibility of the Cabinet Office, departments must generally identify their own recruitment needs. The Civil Service offers guidance to departments on monitoring employment equality and diversity (Civil Service 2015).

If vacancies arise for a particular post, whether in finance or another area, departments are required to follow a specified decision path. The first stage is establishing whether someone internal would like to apply (annex 3D); all vacancies are thus advertised on the Civil Service jobs website. Previously the Civil Service required staff to "move through the grades," and progression could be quite slow; now internal applicants can apply for any post as long as they meet the requirements. If the vacancy cannot be filled internally, the department can seek external recruits.

In September 2015, the Civil Service launched a new specialist Finance Fast Stream with its first intake of graduates, and there is a Finance Apprenticeship Scheme that has an annual intake. For both, applicants must complete a finance qualification. These schemes are open to current civil servants who are supported by their manager and can meet the entry criteria.

Transfers

To build their careers civil servants may move between departments. PFM staff do so: for example, the Ministry of Defence (MOD) permanent secretary worked for three years as head of what was then the Finance Profession at Her Majesty's (HM) Treasury while still employed as the MOD finance director general; previously he had been director general, corporate services for the Department for Children, Schools and Families. Movement also occurs at more junior levels.

Graduates recruited for the 2015–16 Finance Fast Stream scheme are supported in gaining experience in a number of roles across several departments. This experience is seen as important for acquiring a breadth of experience to support progression to a leadership role within government finance. Similar rotations are provided to graduates entering the new Commercial and Internal Audit Fast Streams.

Annex 3A: Her Majesty's (HM) Treasury Target Operating Model Taxonomy[1]

The government finance function now has a Target Operating Model Taxonomy (see figure A3A.1) that defines three pillars in the organization: decision support, reporting and control, and finance operations. Each of the pillars is subdivided into core management roles; for instance, business partnering and planning both contribute to decision support. Activities that contribute to the roles are further defined, for instance, cost analysis and contract management are two elements of business partnering. Activities are also classified by whether they are, for example, controlled locally or at a more senior level across govern-

Figure A3A.1 HM Treasury Finance Target Operating Model

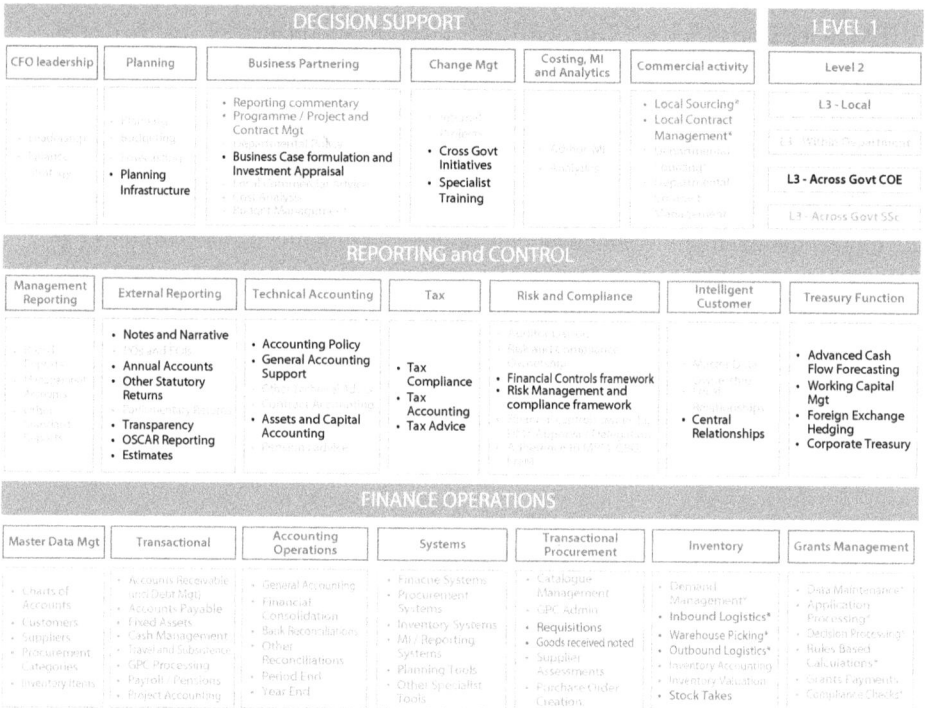

DECISION SUPPORT						LEVEL 1
CFO leadership	Planning	Business Partnering	Change Mgt	Costing, MI and Analytics	Commercial activity	Level 2
	• Planning Infrastructure	• Reporting commentary • Programme / Project and Contract Mgt • Business Case formulation and Investment Appraisal	• Cross Govt Initiatives • Specialist Training		• Local Sourcing* • Local Contract Management*	L3 - Local L3 - Across Govt COE L3 - Across Govt SSc

REPORTING and CONTROL						
Management Reporting	External Reporting	Technical Accounting	Tax	Risk and Compliance	Intelligent Customer	Treasury Function
	• Notes and Narrative • Annual Accounts • Other Statutory Returns • Transparency • OSCAR Reporting • Estimates	• Accounting Policy • General Accounting Support • Assets and Capital Accounting	• Tax Compliance • Tax Accounting • Tax Advice	• Financial Controls framework • Risk Management and compliance framework	• Central Relationships	• Advanced Cash Flow Forecasting • Working Capital Mgt • Foreign Exchange Hedging • Corporate Treasury

FINANCE OPERATIONS						
Master Data Mgt	Transactional	Accounting Operations	Systems	Transactional Procurement	Inventory	Grants Management
• Charts of Accounts • Customers • Suppliers • Procurement Categories • Inventory Items	• Accounts Receivable and Debt Mgt • Accounts Payable • Fixed Assets • Cash Management • Travel and Subsistence • GPC Processing • Payroll, Pensions • Project Accounting	• General Accounting • Financial Consolidation • Bank Reconciliations • Other Reconciliations • Period End • Year End	• Finance Systems • Procurement Systems • Inventory Systems • MI Reporting Systems • Planning Tools • Other Specialist Tools	• Catalogue Management • GPC Admin • Requisitions • Goods received noted • Supplier Assessments • Purchase Order Creation	• Demand Management* • Inbound Logistics* • Warehouse Picking* • Outbound Logistics* • Inventory Accounting • Inventory Valuation • Stock Takes	• Data Maintenance* • Application Processing* • Decision Processing* • Rules Based Calculations* • Grants Payments* • Compliance Checks*

Note: CBG = Consolidated Budgeting Guidance, the latest version of which can be found at: https://www.gov.uk/government/publications/consolidated-budgeting-guidance-2016-to-2017; COE = Centres of Excellence for specialized finance skills of which there are four: Costing, Tax, Investment Appraisal, and Technical Accounting; FOI = (requests for information under the) Freedom of Information Act 2000. The Freedom of Information Act provides public access to information held by public authorities. It does this in two ways: public authorities are obliged to publish certain information about their activities; and. members of the public are entitled to request information from public authorities; FReM = UK Government's Finance Reporting Manual, the latest version of which can be found at: https://www.gov.uk/government/uploads/system/uploads/attachment_data/file/488328/2015-16_FReM__December_2015_.pdf; GPC = Government Procurement Card, similar to a credit card given to authorized officials in central government departments. The card is considered a convenient and cost-effective way to make low-value purchases. Each central government department operates its own card programs, setting policies and controls to ensure staff use cards appropriately; HM = Her Majesty's; HMT = Her Majesty's Treasury; MI = Management Information; MPM = Managing Public Money—a handbook that sets out the main principles for managing resources in the UK public sector organizations; OSCAR = Online System for Central Accounting and Reporting; PQ = Parliamentary Questions—Members of Parliament can ask questions of departments directly (written) or in parliament (tend to be oral); SSc = Shared Service Centre—the government transferred "back office" activities to independent shared service centres across many government departments and their related bodies. The centres carry out high volume processing of, for example, payment transactions for many departments and their allied bodies. The centres are not co-located with the departments.

ment. The Operating Model Taxonomy highlights the interrelationship and dependencies of different activities and roles and the continued importance of internal control and scrutiny.

Finance trainees in the Civil Service are allocated to a particular finance specialty, such as accounts. In some departments that will be their "home" area for the first 18 months, but within that time they will gain short work experience in other areas. Some departments have a home area that lasts beyond that period. With the introduction of the Fast Stream the route through the work experience across government will be more structured.

Finance trainees allocated to departments travel through the broad sphere of Finance, carrying out work experience in at least each of the three pillar areas. Some of the more advanced trainees will work in budgeting and forecasting alongside analysts, economists, statisticians, and subject-specific policy budget managers. While there is a set group of subjects they must experience to meet qualification needs, the order in which they do so is not necessarily set in stone. And all staff can ask to gain experience in particular subject areas. Work experience in any one subject area may vary, but the average time is about six weeks.

Annex 3B: The Role of the Finance Business Partner

The finance business partner (FBP) is a demanding role for traditional finance staff. According to the Treasury government finance function definition, an FBP

- has strong technical skills
- acts strategically and with insight
- influences good decision-making
- thinks commercially and effects change.

The government finance function also defines what managers can expect FBPs to do to help them make decisions:

- communicate very clearly and in a timely manner
- take the time to understand the manager's business
- mix support and challenge to help the manager identify options, issues, and risks
- present insightful information to stimulate longer-term thinking.

This role is based on the FBP role in business and commerce. The government finance function publishes a guide for staff assuming this role.

FBP is becoming more developed in government. The work of FBPs makes for better quality analysis and information in the business context. Budget managers are becoming more accustomed to the idea that finance is an ally rather than an inhibitor.

As an example the following is an extract for a British Council FBP vacancy posting:

Purpose of job: The FBP is the main point of contact for Senior Management, Account Directors and Corporate Finance for all queries relating to the portfolio or projects they support. The portfolio will include global programs. There is a strong emphasis on partnering with managers of those business areas not just to provide consistent, timely, accurate and relevant financial information but more importantly, interpretation and decision support resulting from trends identified in terms of the achievement of strategic business objectives.

The role-holder will be a person with strong knowledge of large international organizations with multiple product / service / geographic business channels and the demands of an organization that is changing in terms of building a larger proportion of income from commercial trading. The role-holder will help British Council business leaders focus on cost management, business development, efficiency improvements, investments, service, and process quality and provide advice on how to reinvest surpluses in support of its purpose. Role-holders will integrate their activities with, and support the aims of, the Global Finance Change and other relevant change initiatives and contribute to achieving successful outcomes.

Annex 3C: Trainee Accountancy Allowance and Progression Arrangements (see GFP 2014)

Example: Ministry of Justice

The Ministry of Justice is one of the largest government departments. For 2014 it offered seven graduate trainee accountant places, all London-based. All places

Figure A3C.1 Allowance Paid to Trainee

Stage	ACCA	CIMA	CIPFA	ICAEW	Additional Reward
On joining scheme	–	–	–	–	Nil
On completion of stage 1	Fundamentals Knowledge	Certificate	Certificate	Knowledge Modules	Nil
On completion of stage 2	Fundamentals Skills	Managerial Level	Diploma Level	Application Modules	Allowance: £1,050 (national) £1,500 (inner London)
On completion of stage 3	Professional Stage	Strategic Level and T4	Final Test of Professional Competence	Advanced Stage	Allowance increase to £2,100 (national) £3,000 (inner London)
On qualification	Fully Qualified with Letters	Fully Qualified with Letters	Fully Qualified with Letters	Fully Qualified with Letters	Allowance increase to £3,150 (national) £5,000 (inner London)

Note: ACCA = Chartered Association of Certified Accountants; CIMA = Chartered Institute of Management Accountants; CIPFA = Chartered Institute of Public Finance and Accountancy; ICAEW = Institute of Chartered Accountants in England and Wales; – = not available; T4 is the "Test of Professional Competence in Management Accounting," the final exam stage for the CIMA professional qualification.

involve a variety of financial management roles in business partnering, financial planning and strategy, performance management, project and program finance, financial accounting, and corporate reporting. There were opportunities in both the administrative center of the Ministry and operationally.

Qualification for entry to this training is a minimum lower second-class degree. Graduates follow a three- to four-year program of study for a professional accountancy qualification. The Ministry

- covers the full cost of study, including initial registration with the professional institute and training provider, materials, tuition, examination, exemption fees, and annual institute membership subscription.
- provides leave for study, including training days, revision courses, and the examination.
- provides a qualified accountancy mentor throughout the period of study and early career, and an accountancy trainee "buddy" (a more experienced trainee) to give informal support through the training course and initial period in the Ministry.

The accountancy and finance institutes accredit the Ministry's finance function training scheme, which opens additional avenues of support. The Ministry has partnering arrangements with key training providers, which can offer access to other support, such as advice.

Students are given a program of work placements so that they gain the practical experience they need to meet the work requirements for the professional qualifications. The Ministry's finance function training scheme provides additional development and networking opportunities, including sponsorship to cross-government events.

The final one-time allowance payable (£5,000) when the individual gains a qualification compares favorably to the position for a similar individual qualifying in the following departments:

- Department for Culture Media and Sport offers a final allowance of £4,000.
- Department for Communities and Local Government offers a final allowance of £1,980.

Annex 3D: Civil Service Resourcing Vacancy Filling Scheme (VFS) (Civil Service Resourcing 2015)

This scheme aims to make better use of scarce and specialist resources across the Civil Service, reduce external recruitment, and give departments access to a much wider labor market. Sharing opportunities and allowing free movement of labor increases the chance of achieving this aim.

The VFS allows any civil servant living or working in a region to apply for any advertised permanent vacancy regardless of grade or department, provided they have the competencies required for the role. If the application is successful, the transfer is permanent and the applicant must accept the terms offered by the recruiting department. The scheme fills vacancies in this sequence:

- Stage 1: Internal, level moves (not a compulsory stage under VFS)
- Stage 2: Exclusive 10-day period for surplus staff in all departments at their current grade
- Stage 3: Vacancies advertised to staff in all departments and accredited non-departmental public bodies, regardless of grade
- Stage 4: External recruitment

Departments can advertise within the entire Civil Service at Stage 1 on promotion or at Stage 3 on level transfer where there is an exceptional business need and approval within the department has been granted.

The scheme applies to any level moves that a department needs to make to accommodate its own business needs. Departments can still run promotions boards and assessment centers for internal candidates. Departments are encouraged to open up promotion opportunities to people from other departments at the earliest opportunity.

In most departments, the approval of the Secretary of State is required for "exceptional business need cases." Departments may have a business reason to offer vacancies more widely. Under VFS, departments *must* openly advertise regional vacancies to all civil servants living or working in the region regardless of grade or department.

No Civil Service departments may opt out. When a civil servant leaves a post, departments need to consider whether a replacement is required. Surplus staff get priority for jobs.

Departments decide what the job requirements are. If the job on offer is for a risk manager, then it would be legitimate to say only qualified risk managers could apply. Departments cannot block promotions.

It is still possible for the department to opt for direct recruitment if there is a business need for the post and internal candidates do not have the competencies it requires. Departments may also be able to solicit external applications for specialist skills if they have conducted internal job advertisements outlining the essential qualifications, skills, and experience required to ensure that only suitable candidates apply while maximizing staff opportunities and optimizing use of specialist skills within the Civil Service.

Note

1. Information about the model (and figure A3A.1) Courtesy Her Majesty's (HM) Treasury. The Target Operating Model was launched at a Government Finance and Internal Audit Event in January 2016.

CHAPTER 4

Professional Development Processes

Career Planning and Management

In the longer term, the aim is to build a community of high-quality public financial management (PFM) professionals who will work in a wide range of government roles. The Civil Service Reform Plan specifies an intention to adopt a corporate approach to managing the career development of those employees with the highest potential.

Civil Service High Potential Stream

In its Capabilities Plan for the Civil Service (annex 4A), the Cabinet Office envisages a more "corporate approach" to building capabilities[1] across the whole Civil Service (Civil Service 2013a). The ambition of Civil Service Talent, the unit that manages the high-potential stream, is to coordinate how the Civil Service manages talent across government departments so as to attract and retain the best talent. The Capabilities Plan introduces the concept of a corporate talent pool, which has been realized as the Civil Service High Potential Stream, which is central to the government's talent approach: For the first time a corporate talent pool will bridge the gap between the Fast Stream entrants and the Top 200 (director general and permanent secretary roles). The High Potential Stream will support those who have the potential to go further and faster than their peers in achieving their career goals and allow the very best talent in the Civil Service to be deployed to organizational priorities. In future, the High Potential Stream will be the route by which internal candidates build their skills and abilities to be the Top 200 of tomorrow. Leaders at every level are responsible for delivering this plan:

- Permanent secretaries will build capability throughout the Civil Service, not just in their departments, and will work together to identify, manage, and deploy talented people from all backgrounds.
- Heads of profession will take a larger role in building capabilities across all areas of the Civil Service.

- Senior civil servants will support individuals who are taking responsibility for their own development.
- All managers will take the time to support their staff in building their individual skills and professional competencies

Fast Track Apprenticeship Scheme

The Fast Track Apprenticeship Scheme gives talented school-leavers an opportunity to work in finance in government. Nongraduates who have achieved a minimum standard can also apply. Individuals enter the scheme through training with the Association of Accounting Technicians (AAT) or Chartered Institute of Management Accountants (CIMA) and progressing through a structured training program for two years while carrying out work assignments. The trainees receive time off during the workweek for study (they also study during evenings and weekends). When the apprenticeship ends, the trainees have acquired a range of skills relevant to PFM, and they are eligible for graduate career jobs.

A highly capable individual could progress from beginning Level 4 AAT or CIMA to completing the professional qualification at a younger age than a graduate taking a degree and embarking on the path to a professional qualification post-degree. The Fast Track program thus makes it possible for a young person to receive professional training that is equivalent to a degree while earning a salary and not being burdened with student debt.

Graduate Fast Stream. Graduate entry to PFM via the Fast Stream entry route is outlined in detail in annex 2L. The same graduate Fast Stream process is used for entry to the Commercial, Project Delivery, and Internal Audit professions. The selection process is rigorous and competitive. Testing covers numerical and verbal reasoning and such behavioral competencies as setting direction, engaging people, and delivering results. Initial shortlisting is based on online testing; that is followed by tests and interviews at an assessment center.

There is no age limit for entry to the Fast Streams, and it does not matter how long ago the candidates graduated, though they are expected to serve for several years before retirement. Fast Streamers are given responsibility quickly. There is a dedicated Civil Service Learning and Development Pathway to support them that includes formal and on-the-job training, feedback and performance reviews, a mentor, and opportunities to attend relevant events such as conferences. By the end of the program, individuals can demonstrate a range of skills and knowledge in such areas as people, financial management, or commercial management and project and program management. Fast Stream candidates who apply directly from university are encouraged to widen their experience before joining the Civil Service in order to develop as rounded individuals, for example by carrying out volunteer work. The Civil Service Fast Stream route is ranked among the top five in *The Times* Top 100 Graduate Employers and has attracted considerable interest: 38,175 people registered on the Fast Stream website in the 2015 competition.

The Civil Service is using innovative ways to widen the pool of applicants for the Fast Stream. Civil Service Resourcing (CSR) took on management of all Fast Stream recruitment in 2011 and launched the 2013 scheme. To increase diversity in the entry cohort, advertisements designed to appeal to nontraditional applicants are placed on the Internet and on social media sites.

Accelerated CIMA and CIPFA Training

Chartered Institute of Public Finance and Accountancy (CIPFA) and CIMA both offer accelerated routes to qualification. CIMA allows access to its Gateway route on the basis of experience rather than academics for experienced professionals working in government. Candidates are supported through a bespoke program to prepare them for the Gateway exam before going on to complete the full qualification. A pilot group from Her Majesty's (HM) Treasury policy team cleared the Gateway in January 2016 and is now working on the final stage of the qualification. This move supports the government's goals of improving collaboration between policy and finance and ensuring that all senior managers demonstrate that they understand finance before they can be eligible for promotion to the highest grades.

CIPFA offers a Certificate in Central Government Finance which allows exemptions from three modules of a full qualification. This certificate targets those in roles, such as those on HM Treasury spending teams, where they would benefit from greater financial understanding and skills but do not necessarily want a full finance qualification. The third cohort will launch in February 2016. A number of people in the previous cohorts who successfully completed the certificate are now moving to convert the certificate into a full CIPFA qualification through the accelerated route.

The Civil Service Capabilities Plan (annex 4A) is designed to move away from the tradition that certain professions were more equal than others by encouraging diversity of experience and skills for most senior managers. The Capabilities Plan (Civil Service 2013a) outlines a set of expectations for particularly ambitious senior managers from any of the professions; for example, they should:

- have a broad range of experience and build their skills as set out in the Competency Framework and the Capabilities Plan;
- move out of a department to gain experience in another sector, which will be seen as a strength, not a diversion; and
- build a diverse career background, for example, combining experience in project delivery, digital service delivery, and commercial work as well as policy.

A number of career management activities supplement the core career path for this talent stream. A pilot for centrally managed secondments for senior civil servants started in May 2013. There are also opportunities for recently qualified staff to take short secondments—for example, a recently qualified finance professional CIMA from the Department for Education received a six-month secondment to Ernst & Young in the private sector. A new High Potential Interchange Scheme is managed centrally by the Cabinet Office.

External Recruitment

The Civil Service Commission regulates recruitment, providing assurance that appointments are on merit after fair and open competition. It also helps promote the Civil Service values of honesty, integrity, objectivity, and impartiality and hears complaints under the Civil Service Code. The Commission is independent of government and the Civil Service. For financial management the Civil Service has entry routes for those who are

- school leavers: the Finance Apprenticeship Scheme;
- graduates: the Finance Fast Stream 2015–16 (a rebranding of the Financial Management Development Scheme, the previous graduate entry route); and
- those who are qualified and part-qualified.

Internal Recruitment

It is very important to us that we are able to bring in talent from wherever it is within the Civil Service. People already working in the Civil Service can apply for the above external routes, but they also have available to them a range of other entry routes, to suit the different career stages and prior experiences of individuals from different backgrounds.

The Civil Service is committed to investing in its people. In 2011–12[2] it invested £178 million (about £425 per civil servant) in formal learning and development opportunities to help people to perform their work better.

All civil servants are expected to take responsibility for their own development. This means working with their line manager to build the skills for their current job and their future career. The core Civil Service Competency Framework (Civil Service 2012a) is there to inform recruitment processes and help with discussions on performance and development. Civil Service Human Resources (HR) Resourcing is responsible for the core framework, although the finance function has contributed by adding a competency to this core framework to recognize the importance of value for money (VfM) concepts and skills for all civil servants. Departments like the Ministry of Defence (MOD) and the Department for Work and Pensions (DWP) previously tailored the core framework to the individual PFM disciplines in their departments. According to the deputy head of government internal audit, not all PFM specialists agree that this is necessary in the Civil Service; professional institutes often have their own competency frameworks for members. The commercial profession has its own Commercial Competency Framework (CCS 2014a) to reflect specific technical skills the role demands. The project delivery profession uses the core Civil Service Competency Framework.

The competency frameworks distinguish different levels of behaviors and skills that individuals require as they progress toward senior management. The totality of training needs is collated and held by each department's HR function, which then submits bids to the department's administrative budget to fund the training.

Training and Development—Design and Delivery

The government finance function is committed to promoting learning and development to ensure that financial professionals have the right skills and capabilities to do their jobs and enhance their careers. It has a range of professional standards and frameworks. Professional institutes are selected for training when their curricula meet the needs of the Civil Service.

Civil servants complete a period of probation after recruitment. Probation policy varies by department, and passing generally means that the individual has met the required standard of conduct, performance, and attendance. In taking this approach, the government draws on the experience of Singapore, making sure that all civil servants must take courses on getting the basics right, including public finance (Civil Service 2014).

Civil servants are encouraged to maintain and refresh their knowledge and skills through continuing professional development (CPD). All civil servants must have five days of CPD a year (annex 4B), which may be formal training or e-learning—and all departments allow some time off for training. For civil servants who are professionally qualified, accountancy institutes specify their own CPD requirements. Civil servants can access a variety of training materials through Civil Service Learning, which acts as a centralized service for departments to obtain most of the core training for their staff and make better use of government's combined purchasing power.[3] Framework contracts can also be used to obtain tailored or off-the-shelf training as required. Individuals can access e-learning at their desks through their e-mail accounts, and their learning activity is recorded to support further development opportunities. The courses are evaluated through staff feedback forms completed at the end of a course.

Across departments the view is widely held that there are gaps in certain skills among finance staff already in post—for example, in commercial and soft skills, such as persuasion and presentation skills—and some departments have decided to create their own programs to address this need. Having identified gaps in skills related to managing and detecting fraud, the Cabinet Office introduced fraud awareness training to better tackle waste through fraud; by February 2015 some 250,000 civil servants had completed the course (Cabinet Office 2015c). A wide range of learning opportunities is available through dedicated internal "academies" run either centrally or by departments. For example, the Commercial Services Centre established a Commissioning Academy (Cabinet Office 2016a) to help senior managers (annex 2B) to better grasp commercial issues when commissioning others to deliver public services. A new Finance Academy was launched in January 2016 to build capability across government as one response to the Financial Management Review recommendations. The Finance Academy will provide a coherent learning and development option for individuals who work in government finance. The academy is initially directing its attention to a few priority areas, such as Finance Business Partnering (annex 3B) and Commercial Skills for Finance Professionals.

Employers and students both get feedback on the student's progress from Consultative Committee of Accountancy Bodies (CCAB) institutes and training providers. During performance appraisals individuals meet with the line manager to discuss development plans and CPD needs. Departments monitor satisfaction with the quality and relevance of the training provided to their team members.

The Civil Service is taking PFM professional development training more seriously; it believes that both departments and individuals benefit from different types of training. Most of the discussion so far has been about training new civil servants (except for the Commissioning Academy), but there is also a range of learning sources to meet the recognized needs of senior civil servants and non-executive directors joining public sector management boards or audit committees. (GIAA issued a revised *Audit and Risk Assurance Committee Handbook* in March 2016 [GIAA 2016a]). An example is the emergence of the Public Chairs Forum—a group of those who chair department arm's-length bodies who share good practices and discuss concerns, feeding into policy and senior management at the center and publishing guidance for senior managers.[4] There is also targeted leadership training, mentors, and a Civil Service Project Leaders Network (Cabinet Office 2015c), established in March 2012 for peer support and sharing of best practices. Civil Service Learning is working with training suppliers to launch a new leadership academy for senior civil servants—a move urged by Member of Parliaments (MPs) who were concerned that top officials were "not getting access to the sort of training they require" to confront the "unique challenges faced by public service leaders" (Foster 2016a)

The commitment to development extends to the leadership of the Civil Service. After the summer of 2016, civil servants applying for Permanent Secretary posts will be expected to show that they have the right mix of skills by having completed an appropriate business school leadership program in finance, project management, or another subject related to financial management. The government is considering how to ensure that the talent pipeline for such posts has the right mix of commercial and transformational capabilities (Civil Service 2014).

Departments actively use short periods of work experience in different areas of PFM as a cost-effective way to build PFM knowledge, skills, and understanding of front-line service delivery. For example, in the DWP individuals may apply through their manager to shadow a colleague on the front line of service delivery.

Annex 4A: The Civil Service Capabilities Plan[5]

This is the first time that a Capabilities Plan has been published for the whole Civil Service (Cabinet Office 2013). Because the U.K. Civil Service serves three governments, the national government in Westminster and the governments of Scotland and Wales, it must ensure it meets the needs of each.[6] The plan outlines the work proposed to address skill deficiencies in four priority areas for delivering better public services. It establishes a new, more corporate, approach to building on current capabilities, embedding it for the first time in a more rigorous competency framework and performance management system.

The plan is about people and skills—how individuals are trained and their competencies heightened. The intent is that all civil servants will be equipped with the tools and skills they need to deliver more effectively. The plan also considers how the Civil Service can structure, manage, and deploy skills to maximize their potential. It sets out the role of senior managers, what needs to happen at the center (corporate level), and what departments and individuals need to do to build the capabilities required.

Actions to Implement the Plan

The Capabilities Plan addresses the concern that the Civil Service has been largely operating in departmental silos, reducing its effectiveness in sharing expert resources across government and limiting its ability to build organizational capability in specialist skills. The plan identifies four areas where action is required to strengthen capabilities. Actions required in the center of government are distinguished from those required in the departments. The actions required are defined in terms of

- Leading and managing change
- Commercial skills and behaviors
- Delivering special projects and programs
- Redesigning services and delivering them digitally.

The capability gaps in these four areas are to be met by a combination of building internal capabilities through learning and development for current civil servants; bringing in from outside more people with the missing skills to help deliver on the government's digital, project, and commercial capabilities priorities; and borrowing skills through more loans between departments and secondments with private organizations.

The plan recognizes that the Civil Service needs to be representative of the public it serves and encourages a more diverse and inclusive Civil Service to improve organizational capability. It introduces the new core Competency Framework for the Civil Service that defines how civil servants should work (in terms of behaviors) and categorizes the work of civil servants in three leadership behaviors: setting direction, engaging people, and delivering results. The framework provides the foundation for performance management and development planning. Because managers are key to its use, it is important that departments ensure that managers give constructive feedback and help those on their team to improve their skills. The framework captures the four capability priorities in the plan, integrating them into the description of the skills and behaviors required for individuals to succeed at every level in the Civil Service.

Measuring Success

The plan identifies a number of measures of success:

- The Civil Service tracks both measures of staff engagement[7] and specific indicators, including skills, learning and development, diversity, and leadership and management of change. The Civil Service carries out an annual People Survey to assess the attitudes and work-life experiences of staff. Over 279,000 people (representing about two-thirds of the Civil Service and 101 entities within it) took part in the 2015 Survey and 240,000 people did so in 2014 (Heywood 2014; annex 5A describes a selection of key measures of staff engagement).
- Departments keep management information. If skills are improved the impact should be measurable through changes in efficiency: for instance, the time it takes Finance to prepare accounts for publication is decreasing, with most accounts now prepared ahead of the parliamentary recess.
- Being collated now are data on the number of training days completed by individuals and in departments and their satisfaction with the training received, though the data are not yet readily available.
- Departments are preparing workforce plans to identify such Human Resources (HR) information as that related to recruitment and retention and individual competency assessments. This work will take time because information must be pulled from the many legacy systems across government.
- Professions in departments like the Department for Work and Pensions (DWP) are also collecting information to identify the level of professional skills, including the number of people with a certain qualification or experience.

Among the new tools departments are using to evaluate progress are

- An annual skills review that is a light-touch assessment by departments, supported by Civil Service Learning. It aims to identify new and emerging requirements. After its first year, it will also provide a baseline for gauging progress in closing skills gaps.
- A Departmental Improvement Planning model introduced in all departments in 2014 focused on capabilities.
- An independent external assessment of achievement against the plan was begun in 2015.
- Single departmental plans spanning 2015–16 were published in February 2016.[8]

Leaders at all levels will receive increased scrutiny in their own appraisals of what they are doing to build capability. Tools here include 360-degree feedback to allow individuals to measure their progress.

Annex 4B: Continuing Professional Development

All civil servants are being encouraged to maintain their professional knowledge and skills through a variety of different routes. The Civil Service Guide recommends five days a year of pursuing activities to support and develop staff careers. Many short courses and other events are available through Civil Service Learning Gateway, which is open to all civil servants. Other activities may include short secondments to a different business area or a period shadowing the work of a more senior colleague.

The Finance Academy is also developing a program of learning and events specifically tailored to the requirements of central Finance staff. The various Finance Institutes have slightly different guidance and requirements for qualified professionals; it is up to civil servants to ensure that they meet the requirements of the institute they choose. Some may require individuals to carry out a defined annual minimum quantity of continuous professional development (CPD) training hours, which may exceed the 5 days suggested by the Civil Service Guide, and may also describe the types of training that would meet their requirements. Other institutes are less prescriptive, instead emphasizing the need for individuals to focus on the quality of their learning and, after discussion with their managers, its relevance to their immediate and future development.

The Procurement Profession has its own curriculum that details learning opportunities relevant to everyone within the profession. Other professional learning and development opportunities are available through a department's own formal training or through informal on-the-job training, coaching and mentoring.[9]

The Internal Audit Profession maintains a website on Civil Service Learning for those who wish to engage with its professional community and find out about the learning, qualifications, and opportunities available to build skills.

Notes

1. *Capabilities* is the term the Cabinet Office uses to describe the coming together of structures, processes, and skills to deliver outcomes.
2. Latest figures available, Cabinet Office website.
3. The Civil Service Learning contract was renewed as of March 2016. The structure of the contract was not finalized at the time of this report (see Foster 2016b).
4. The Public Chairs Forum exists to improve the efficiency and effectiveness of the delivery of public services in the United Kingdom. It is a member-led, exclusive information sharing and networking resource for chairs of public bodies. www.public-chairsforum.org.uk/

5. http://my.civilservice.gov.uk/reform/skilled/the-civil-service-capabilities-plan/6-overview-of-actions-to-implement-the-plan/ NB. This précis does not include all actions proposed within the plan.

6. The Northern Ireland Civil Service has been a separate organization since 1921.

7. https://civilservice.blog.gov.uk/2014/11/20/the-people-survey-your-views-and-the-results-that-count/

8. All Single Departmental Plans are available from the Cabinet Office, https://www.gov.uk/government/collections/single-departmental-plans-for-2015-to-2020. (It is not clear whether these will be in addition to or replace the Departmental Improvement plans.)

9. https://www.gov.uk/government/organisations/civil-service-procurement-profession/about#career-opportunities-and-professional-development.

CHAPTER 5

Results and Indicators

Attraction and Retention

The various professional entry schemes seem to have been successful in attracting suitable applicants, but because the program is still expanding the results are preliminary. The first recruitment for the new Civil Service Fast Track Apprenticeship Scheme attracted 2,519 applications for 30 positions. All were filled, and the apprentices started work in September 2014.

Overall, departments identified a need for some 71 graduates to join the Financial Management Training and Development Scheme for 2014–15.[1] Considering the success in recruiting graduates for 2013 and high graduate interest in fast track entry to the Civil Service in general, the departments should be able to recruit the graduates they require. Interest in the Fast Stream is considerable: 38,175 people registered on the Fast Stream website in the 2015 competition.[2]

Some 80 experienced senior finance professional civil servants who did not previously hold a professional accountancy qualification and were completing the fast track development scheme for finance for a Chartered Institute of Public Finance and Accountancy (CIPFA) qualification were successfully trained through Warwick University.

Starting in 2015–16, the three core public financial management (PFM) disciplines—finance, audit, and commercial—are being added to the core Civil Service Fast Stream program. In September 2015, 49 individuals were appointed to the Finance Fast Stream (figures were not available for the Internal Audit and Commercial specialist schemes).

New graduates for procurement positions for 2015–16 were recruited through the Civil Service Commercial Fast Stream and a new Commercial Fast Track apprenticeship scheme (CCS 2015, 28). For senior commercial capability officers there is a Commercial Recruitment Hub based in the Cabinet Office.

How candidates are recruited for posts in internal audit is slightly less clear. The original department-based audit groups varied considerably in size and profile. Until the move to shared services is finalized, the position on vacancies will remain uncertain. Two graduates were recruited through the Internal Audit Profession route in 2014 for Her Majesty's (HM) Revenue and Customs and the Driver and Vehicle Licencing Agency. Although specialist skills, such as computer audit, are in short supply, these skills can be contracted or supported through shared-service arrangements.

Mobility continues to be a problem: finance staff tended to remain in one post too long. To address this, central government departments are drafting workforce plans and talent management strategies. For example, the policy of the Department for Work and Pensions policy is that for development purposes, individuals should move within three years. At the same time, the departments must also seek to maintain a balance of experience and knowledge.

Skills and Competencies

The Civil Service is working to track the career details (work experience, formal training, etc.) of each staff member as part of the government's determination to proactively identify people who would meet the requirements of unfilled PFM vacancies, particularly specialist vacancies, on short notice. This will take time.

A number of qualified finance professionals work outside mainstream finance (figure 5.1). They may work in nonfinance roles, gaining business knowledge and understanding. They may be moving across functions to gain a rounded set of skills and experience for progression to senior management. That the number is constant suggests that the Civil Service is able to retain PFM specialists with financial skills. This may not continue to be true once the job market changes.

Some qualifications, such as Institute of Chartered Accountants in England and Wales (ICAEW; a more recent route for graduates to enter the public sector), can give individuals particularly attractive career options in both the private and the public sector. When the external economy is strong, it may be difficult to retain

Figure 5.1 Finance Staff Working Outside Mainstream Finance, 2009–13

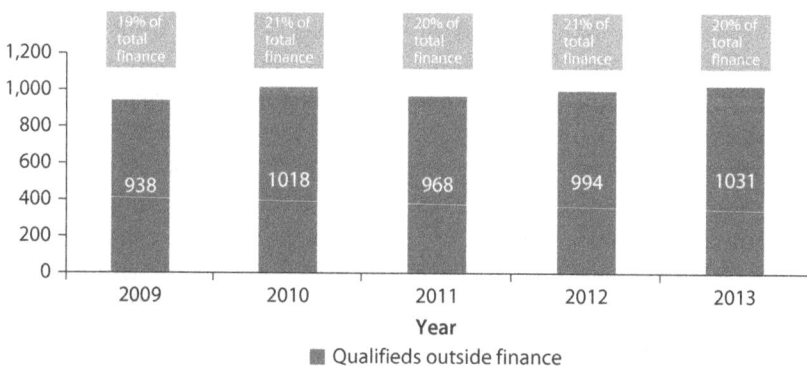

Source: Finance Staff Survey 2013, HM Treasury.

them. CIPFA graduates also find opportunities in both sectors, though the attrition rates are lower and during the austerity period departures have declined. Some departments (e.g., Ministry of Justice and Ministry of Defence[MOD]) have introduced a clause in their contracts to the effect that graduates who are training for a professional qualification with the organization should not leave within two years after receiving the qualification; this measure ensures that some value is returned to the training department.

The government finance function has also started to recruit directly rather than through departments (Russell 2016, 23). Ten deputy directors were recently recruited, of whom seven came from the wider public sector or private enterprise. There is also a focus on recruiting people at mid-career level because the Treasury recognizes it can be difficult for an individual to arrive in a senior role without some exposure to the politics and culture of working with ministers.

The October 2014 Civil Service Reform Plan Progress Report stated that the most critical skills gaps remaining were in commercial and contract management. A Commercial Recruitment Hub has therefore been set up to attract and deploy talent. In its first campaign 30 senior vacancies in six government departments were filled, and 68 percent of the new hires were from the private sector. As part of recruitment in 2014–15, the Senior Civil Service cadre went from 18 to 56, bringing more senior and experienced staff into key positions. In an extension of the work to recruit expertise, a number of senior commercial leaders from industry are now working as Crown Representatives, helping government to act as a single customer, building close relationships between government and strategic suppliers, and securing savings on major procurement programs. The Crown Commercial Services (CCS) has also forged links with universities and put in place an interchange program with industry.

In addition to bringing in senior professionals from outside, Civil Service Learning has new learning offers and core curricula (for those skills common throughout Whitehall) in key PFM priority areas for all civil servants. The aim is to ensure that the training on offer is co-created with civil servants so that it reflects their needs, and delivered by people who are best in class and experts in their areas. "We want learning which properly reflects the context in which civil servants are operating, so that it has some elements of being tailored and personalised to what civil servants want to learn and how they want to learn it" (Foster 2016b). This initiative stimulated a high demand for learning in these areas (see Table 5.1). A further result is that the government plans to double the size of the Commissioning Academy to meet a target of 1,500 participants by 2016.[3]

The government planned to assess whether the measures to recruit and train individuals in commercial skills are having the intended impact at the end of the 2014–15 financial year and issued a refreshed competency self-assessment tool for departments to complete a second skills assessment at a later date. The intent is to identify the extent to which the skills gap has been closed in priority capability areas.

Table 5.1 Completion of Courses in Priority Capability Areas

	2013–14 Quarter 2	2013–14 Quarter 3[a]	2013–14 Quarter 4
Commercial skills	7,190	13,685	26,055
Project and program management skills	984	2,813	6,168

Source: HM Treasury.

[a]In November 2013, part way through quarter 3, the Civil Service introduced new learning opportunities in these areas.

In relation to training on management of major projects, by the end of 2014, about 340 staff had attended the Major Projects Leadership Academy. In April 2015–16, the training extended to the next generation of project and program managers to further embed project delivery skills. After one year, the Infrastructure and Projects Authority is deemed to have had a real measurable impact: whereas previously just 30 percent of projects were likely to deliver on time and at budget, today more than 60 percent are. However, further work is considered necessary to ensure that projects run effectively. The government has started to execute a talent management strategy for academy graduates to make best use of their new skills across the government's major projects portfolio. The success of the Major Projects Leadership Academy (MPLA) is attracting attention around the world, and other governments are emulating its model for training their leaders of major projects. In 2014, the MPLA received a Silver Award from the European Foundation for Management Development in its Excellence in Practice Awards (Cabinet Office 2015e).

Examples of success from the investment in better PFM skills can be drawn from the DWP Finance Group. The improved working papers prepared to support the accounts resulted in more efficient audits and closing of the accounts on June 24, 2013, ahead of the July 18 deadline. Success can also be seen from recognizably better collaboration between finance staff and their commercial colleagues to identify significant savings by negotiating the prices for major contracts. Better collaborative working relationships are also being seen in the preparation of more robust business cases, which are approved more quickly because based on the business cases they meet the information requirements of those approving the projects.

Rewards

Professionalizing PFM raises expectations that pay scales will rise to reflect the increased value that a qualification offers. Finance professionals are valued in the private sector, where pay has traditionally been higher than in the public sector. If pay expectations are not met within a reasonable time after qualification, PFM specialists—particularly those who hold qualifications that are attractive to the private sector, such as Chartered Association of Certified Accountants (ACCA), Chartered Institute of Management Accountants (CIMA), and ICAEW—may leave. During the economic downturn natural attrition rates tended to slow, but they did not disappear completely.

The caliber of civil servants is "generally very high," but the cap on Civil Service pay "is making it difficult to recruit talented staff."[4] Better talent management and rewards for good performance are required. For example, the MOD told the Public Accounts Committee (PAC) in May 2014 that it urgently needed to address the shortage of skills across its critical functions; it needed to be able to pay more to attract and retain people with specialist skills (Parliament 2014).

Entry salaries for professionally qualified PFM civil servants vary by department. Salary ranges for the first post-qualification positions also vary widely (there are no published salary rates); because some departments support fast-track promotion for the very best individuals, it is hard to compare departments. Professional qualifications attract an annual allowance, though again the allowance is not constant across departments for any given qualification. When an individual makes a career move away from the initial profession, for example, from internal audit to one of the operational divisions, the allowance may be removed.

It is often said that individuals do not join the public sector for pay alone. Graduate recruitment application information stresses the whole package of benefits in addition to pay that the individual gains from joining the Civil Service—such as the wide variety in the job and the intellectual challenge. According to the focus group, these elements are considered as important as salary in attracting high-caliber individuals to train with the Civil Service. However, Sir David Normington, First Civil Service Commissioner, voiced a word of caution on building the Civil Service of the future:

> I need to sound a more serious warning about the growing and critical gap between the government's aspiration to transform the skills of the Civil Service at the top levels and the ability to recruit the kind of skills needed. […] We are seriously concerned that without a complete rethink of the current approach to senior pay, the Civil Service will struggle to attract the very skills it needs and may find it harder to retain the talent it already has in critical areas. (Civil Service Commission 2014, Foreword)

For the more senior managers, pay differentials between the public and private sectors become an interesting topic of conversation at the departmental water coolers.[5] For the Civil Service to retain high-performing, highly skilled individuals in the higher echelons will require a combination of stimulating and intellectually demanding opportunities and an attractive benefits package.

Some words of caution also about the challenge ahead. One person interviewed stated that there is a "growing and critical gap between the government's aspiration to transform the skills of the Civil Service at the top levels and the ability to recruit the kind of skills needed." At the same time,

> Some 66,000 full-time staff left the Civil Service since the 2010 review—a headcount reduction of nearly 14 per cent. A further 32,000 posts must go if the

government is to reach the goal of the Civil Service Reform Plan of a Civil Service of some 380,000 staff. The direction of reform adds urgency to the capability challenges facing the Civil Service, particularly in areas such as commercial skills and managing public service markets. Despite staff engagement surveys remaining stable in 2012 and 2013, morale is likely to be tested by further downsizing, restructuring and continuing pressure on pay. (Thomas and Pearson 2014)

Annex 5A provides extracts from the 2015 survey.

Recent National Audit Office (NAO) reports (NAO 2014a, b, and reports cited therein) recorded high staff turnover in the Treasury (25.2 percent in 2011–12 and 22 percent in 2012–13). This level of attrition reflects the ability of high-caliber graduates to command attractive job opportunities even when external economic conditions are difficult. Although the Treasury believes that such staff movement offers opportunities to refresh and maintain skills and expertise, the NAO notes that such a high departure rate raises risks to service quality and efficiency. Civil Service pay awards are limited to 1 percent in 2016, which is likely to further impact attrition rates.[6]

Annex 5A: Civil Service People Survey 2015[7]

The Civil Service conducts an annual survey of its staff (the People Survey) to assess their attitudes and work-life experiences. The 2015 survey drew responses from more than 279,653 people across the Civil Service (Civil Service 2015). The table shows a selection of the 2015 responses to statements relevant to pro-

Figure A5A.1 Civil Service People Survey 2015, Civil Service Benchmark Scores, November 2015

Employee engagement survey statement	2015 Results (%)	Change since 2014 (%)	2009 Results (%)
I can access learning when I want to.	63	+ 1	63
Learning and development opportunities I have taken in the last 12 months have helped me improve performance.	52	+ 1	51
There are opportunities for me to develop my career in [my organization].	41	−1	39
Learning and development activities I have completed while working for [my organization] are helping me to develop my career.	44	+ 1	44
I feel that my pay adequately reflects my performance.	31	+2	36
I am satisfied with the total benefits package.	33	+1	44
Compared to people doing a similar job in other organizations, I feel my pay is reasonable.	25	+1	33
I want to stay working for [my organization] for at least the next three years.	43	−4	55
Overall staff engagement survey index.	58	−1	58

Source: Cabinet Office 2015a.

fessional development and building capacity and capability as they relate to responses in 2014 and 2009.

The result for each of the themes is calculated as the percentage of "strongly agree" or "agree" responses to all questions in that theme. The results suggest a more positive approach to civil servants training than in 2012, with scores regaining the levels seen in 2009 and continuing the upward trend noted for 2014. On the other hand, in terms of opportunities for development of their careers, and more particularly wishing to remain in their organization over the next 3 years, staff would appear to be less positive than they were in both 2009 and 2014, a slight downward trend.

These surveys provide senior management with a useful indication of the impact of change within organizations.

Notes

1. A twice-yearly competitive option to join the Fast Stream is available to all current civil servants below Grade 7 equivalent, whether or not they are in a finance role.

2. In its 2015 survey the Association of Graduate Recruiters (AGR) found that the public sector remains an attractive employer for graduate applications, receiving 44 applications for every vacancy in 2014–15 compared to 22 for every vacancy notified by accountancy or professional services organizations. Page 33, AGR 2015 Annual Survey—FINAL https://www.agr.org.uk.

3. The Senior Civil Servant community has not always been "accepting [of] the importance of learning and capability." Some were considered to be "just paying lip service to this agenda, and didn't really accept the importance of investing in staff learning and development unless it was business critical." The 2012 Civil Service Reform Plan focus on skills and capabilities was "helpful and supportive" in getting Civil Service Learning off the ground. (See Winnie Agbonlahor 2015).

4. http://www.bbc.co.uk/news/uk-politics-18019941 (accessed January 2016).

5. http://www.gov.uk/government/publications/civil-service-pay-guidance-2015-to-2016/civil-service-pay-guidance-2015-to-2016 (accessed March 1, 2016). In the Budget 2013, the government announced that public sector pay awards would be limited to an average of up to 1 percent in 2015 to 2016; and in addition that pay awards for civil service departments who entered the pay freeze early would also average at 1 percent, aligning them with the rest of the public sector.

6. https://www.gov.uk/government/publications/civil-service-pay-guidance-2015-to-2016/civil-service-pay-guidance-2015-to-2016. In Budget 2013, the government announced that public sector pay awards would be limited to an average of up to 1 percent in 2015 to 2016; and in addition that pay awards for civil service departments who entered the pay freeze early would also average 1 percent, aligning them with the rest of the public sector.

7. https://www.gov.uk/government/uploads/system/uploads/attachment_data/file/477335/csps2015_benchmark_report.pdf (accessed February 15, 2016).

Timeline: Developing Professional Finance in Government

Date	Event
1968	Fulton Report examines the structure, recruitment, training, and management of the Home Civil Service.
1982	Exchequer and Audit (later the National Audit Office, NAO) begins a professional training scheme (CIPFA) for new graduates recruited.
1982	Financial Management Initiative (FMI) is started
1982	Government Accountancy Service (GAS) is established, with Ken Sharp as the first head.
1983	National Audit Office Act establishes an independent external audit institution.
1987	Departmental heads of accountancy profession are appointed (later retitled heads of finance professionalism).
1993	Andrew Likierman becomes head of GAS.
2001	Resource accounting and budgeting is introduced, providing a "burning platform" for the professionalization of finance staff.
2003	Principal finance officers become finance directors.
2004	Government Accounting Service Management Unit becomes the Finance Professionalism Team.
2005	Government Hundred Group, a network of finance heads, is convened.
2005	*Corporate Governance Code* (the Code) is published for central government.
2005	Finance is named a core skill under Professional Skills for Government.
2006	GAS becomes the Government Finance Profession.
2006	Finance Skills for All e-learning is launched under Professional Skills for Government.
2006	Cross-government finance graduate recruitment scheme is launched.
2008	Jon Thompson becomes the first professionally trained accountant to be named head of the finance profession.
2010	A cross-government task force is established to tackle fraud and error; debt and grants are later added to its remit.
2010	After its first spending review, the coalition government announces substantial cuts to departmental budgets through 2014–15.
2011	The Major Projects Authority is launched, introducing controls to ensure effective management of large government projects,

table continues next page

Date	Event
2011	"Managing Taxpayers' Money Wisely" is published to set out the intent of the Finance Transformation Programme.
2011	HM Treasury publishes *Corporate Governance in Central Government Departments: Code of Good Practice.*
2012	OSCAR management information system is launched to provide HM Treasury with the data it needs to monitor public spending
2012	The Civil Service Reform Plan is published.
2013	Office of the Government Finance Profession comes into being.
2013	First contract awarded for independent shared service centers to provide back-office services to government departments and "arm's-length" bodies.
2013	NAO publishes its report on *Financial Management in Government.*
2013	HM Treasury publishes *Managing Public Money* to replace the *Government Accounting Manual.*
2013	The Financial Management Review recommends a new joint post of head of public spending and head of Government Finance Profession.
2014	New director general of public spending and finance is appointed in HM Treasury (combining head of public spending and head of government finance profession) New head of government internal audit is appointed, reporting to the director general of spending and finance. New chief executive of the Civil Service is appointed, acting as the accounting officer and line manager for most of the functional professions.
2015	In the *Autumn Spending Review 2015*, the Chancellor commits to "continue to drive up the quality of financial management and the capability of the [renamed] government finance function to deliver its fiscal plan."
2016	Government Finance and Internal Audit 2016 updates staff on the financial management reform program and the future of the finance function. On January 1, 2016, Infrastructure U.K. is merged with the Major Projects Authority to form the Infrastructure and Projects Authority.

References

Agbonlahor, Winnie. 2015. "Jerry Arnott, former chief executive, Civil Service Learning, UK: Exclusive Interview." *Global Government Forum*, August 9, 2015.

Alexander, Danny. 2013. Foreword to *Strengthening Financial Management Capability in Government*. London: HM Treasury.

Allen, David, and Johannes Wolff. 2016. "Understanding Costs to Unlock Opportunities." *Civil Service Quarterly*, January 21, 2016, https://quarterly.blog.gov.U.K./2016/01/21/understanding-costs-to-unlock-opportunities.

Blitz, James. 2013. *"Defence Budget to Carry Over £1.6bn." Financial Times, February 12, 2013.* http://www.ft.com/cms/s/0/5a23d7a4-753e-11e2-a9f3-00144feabdc0.html#axzz41YaUwmrZ.

Brecknell, Susannah. 2014. "PAC Calls for Pay Flexibility to Plug Skill Gaps." *Civil Service World*, May 15, 2014. http://www.civilserviceworld.com/articles/news/pac-calls-pay-flexibility-plug-skill-gaps.

Cabinet Office. n.d. Fast Stream website. https://www.gov.U.K./government/organisations/civil-service-fast-stream.

Cabinet Office. n.d. SCS database.

———. 2009. Assessment of the Capability Review Programme Civil Service. https://www.nao.org.uk/wp-content/uploads/2009/02/0809123es.pdf.

———. 2012. Civil Service Competency Framework 2012–2017. https://www.gov.U.K./government/uploads/system/uploads/attachment_data/file/436073/cscf_fulla4potrait_2013-2017_v2d.pdf.

———. 2013. Meeting the Challenge of Change: A Capabilities Plan for the Civil Service. https://www.gov.U.K./government/uploads/system/uploads/attachment_data/file/307250/Civil_Service_Capabilities_Plan_2013.pdf.

———. 2014. Civil Service Reform Plan: Progress Report, October 2, 2014. https://www.gov.U.K./government/uploads/system/uploads/attachment_data/file/360637/Civil_Service_Reform_Plan_-_Progress_Report__web_.pdf.

———. 2015a. "Civil Service People 2015, Benchmark Scores." https://www.gov.uk/government/uploads/system/uploads/attachment_data/file/477335/csps2015_benchmark_report.pdf.

———. 2015b. "Equality and Diversity." https://www.gov.uk/government/organisations/civil-service/about/equality-and-diversity.

———. 2015c. "Fraud, Error and Debt Conference: Francis Maude Speech." https://www.gov.U.K./government/speeches/fraud-error-and-debt-conference-francis-maude-speech.

————. 2015d. "Government Creates New Body to Help Manage and Deliver Major Projects for UK Economy." Press release. https://www.gov.uk/government/news/government-creates-new-body-to-help-manage-and-deliver-major-projects-for-uk-economy.

————. 2015e. *Major Projects Authority Annual Report 2014–15*. https://www.gov.uk/government/uploads/system/uploads/attachment_data/file/438333/Major_Projects_Authority_Annual_Report_2015.pdf.

————. 2015f. *Major Projects Leadership Academy MPLA Handbook*. https://www.gov.uk/government/uploads/system/uploads/attachment_data/file/405600/MPLA_Handbook_for_gov_uk.pdf.

————. 2016a. "Commissioning Academy Brochure." https://www.gov.uk/government/publications/the-commissioning-academy-brochure.

————. 2016b. "The Commissioning Academy." https://www.gov.uk/the-commissioning-academy-information

CCS (Crown Commercial Service). 2014a. http://webarchive.nationalarchives.gov.uk/20140305122816/http://www.civilservice.gov.uk/networks/gps.

————. 2014b. Commercial and Procurement Training. https://www.gov.uk/commercial-and-procurement-training.

————. 2015. *Annual Report and Accounts, 2014/15*. https://www.gov.uk/government/uploads/system/uploads/attachment_data/file/446765/ccs-annual-report-2014-2015-HC207-web.pdf.

Civil Service. n.d. a. Human Resources Profession Homepage. https://www.gov.uk/government/organisations/civil-service-human-resources-profession/about.

————. n.d. b. "Working for the Civil Service." https://www.gov.uk/government/organisations/civil-service/about/recruitment.

————. n.d. c. Fast Stream Website. https://www.gov.uk/government/organisations/civil-service-fast-stream.

————. n.d. d. Procurement Profession Website. https://www.gov.uk/government/organisations/civil-service-procurement-profession.

————. 2012a. Civil Service Competency Framework 2012–2017. https://www.gov.uk/government/uploads/system/uploads/attachment_data/file/436073/cscf_fulla4portrait_2013-2017_v2d.pdf.

————. 2012b. The Civil Service Reform Plan. https://www.gov.uk/government/publications/civil-service-reform-plan.

————. 2012c. *Civil Service Competency Plan*. As updated in 2015: https://www.gov.uk/government/publications/civil-service-competency-framework

————. 2012d. Government Finance Profession: A celebration of 30 years. GFP in association with CIMA.

————. 2013a. Meeting the Challenge of Change: A Capabilities Plan for the Civil Service. https://www.gov.uk/government/uploads/system/uploads/attachment_data/file/307250/Civil_Service_Capabilities_Plan_2013.pdf.

————. 2013b. Civil Service Reform One Year On. https://www.gov.uk/government/uploads/system/uploads/attachment_data/file/211506/CSR_OYO_LOW_RES_PDF.pdf.

————. 2014. Civil Service Reform Plan: Progress Report, October 2, 2014. https://www.gov.uk/government/uploads/system/uploads/attachment_data/file/360637/Civil_Service_Reform_Plan_-_Progress_Report__web_.pdf.

———. 2015. "The Commercial Core Skills Offer." https://civilservice.blog.gov.uk/wp-content/uploads/sites/86/2015/04/The-Commercial-Core-Skills-Offer_v6.pdf.

Civil Service Commission. 2014. *Annual Report and Accounts, 2013–14, Foreword.* https://www.gov.uk/government/uploads/system/uploads/attachment_data/file/322962/2902194_CSC_AnnualReport_acc.pdf

———. 2015. "Recruitment Principles." http://civilservicecommission.independent.gov.uk/civil-service-recruitment/.

Civil Service Resourcing. 2015. "Vacancy Holder Guidance." https://www.gov.uk/government/uploads/system/uploads/ attachment_data/file/458964/150907-Vacancy_Holder_Guidance_V5.pdf.

Complete University Guide. 2016. "What Do Graduates Earn?" http://www.thecompleteuniversityguide.co.uk/careers/what-do-graduates-do/what-do-graduates-earn/.

Crothers, Bill. 2015. "Launch of the New Civil Service Fast Stream." https://faststream.blog.gov.uk/2015/04/01/launch-of-the-new-civil-service-commercial-fast-stream.

Dunton, Jim. 2016. "Greg Hands Hails 'Impressive Progress' on Treasury's Financial Management Reform Programme." *Civil Service World* January 29, 2016. http://www.civilserviceworld.com/articles/news/greg-hands-hails-%E2%80%9Cimpressive-progress%E2%80%9D-treasury%E2%80%99s-financial-management-reform.

FRC (Financial Reporting Council). 2015a. Changes in the Companies Act 2006 in relation to Recognised Supervisory Bodies (RSBs) https://www.frc.org.uk/Home.aspx.

———. 2015b. Key Facts and Trends in the Accountancy Profession. https://www.frc.org.uk/Our-Work/Publications/Professional-Oversight/Key-Facts-and-Trends-in-the-Accountancy-Profes-(1).pdf.

Freeguard, G., E. Andrews, R. Munro, J. Randall, and D. Devine. 2015. *Whitehall Monitor 2015.* London: Institute for Government.

Foster, Matt. 2016a. "Civil Service Learning Chief Hilary Spencer: Revamped Training Scheme Will Provide a 'Much Better' Digital Service." *Training Journal*, January 15, 2016. https://www.trainingjournal.com/articles/feature/civil-service-learning-chief-hilary-spencer-revamped-training-scheme-will-provide.

———. 2016b. "What Is the Civil Service Doing to Improve Staff Training?" *Training Journal*, February 1, 2016. https://www.trainingjournal.com/articles/feature/what-civil-service-doing-improve-staff-training.

GCF (Government Commercial Function). 2015a. "Commercial Skills and Competency Framework for Developing and Practitioner Levels." https://www.gov.uk/government/uploads/system/uploads/attachment_data/file/501136/Commercial_Skills_Framework_v_October_2015__1_.pdf.

———. 2015b. "Commercial Professional Curriculum Revised." https://www.gov.uk/government/uploads/system/uploads/attachment_data/file/418424/Commercial-Professional-Curriculum-Revised_23_03_15.pdf.

GFP. 2014. "Information for Applicants" (DWP example). https://www.online-jobs.co.U.K./i-grasp/docs/gfp/2014/DWP.pdf.

GIAA. 2015. "About Us" homepage. https://www.gov.uk/government/organisations/government-internal-audit-agency/about.

———. 2016a. *Audit and Risk Assurance Committee Handbook.* https://www.gov.uk/government/uploads/system/uploads/attachment_data/file/512760/PU1934_Audit_committee_handbook.pdf.

———. 2016b. Corporate Plan. https://www.gov.uk/government/publications/government-internal-audit-agency-corporate-plan.

Hands, Greg. 2016. Speech to the Financial Management Reform Conference in Birmingham. https://www.gov.uk/government/speeches/chief-secretary-to-the-treasury-on-financial-management-in-government.

Heywood, Sir Jeremy. 2014. "The People Survey—Your Views and the Results that Count." https://civilservice.blog.gov.uk/2014/11/20/the-people-survey-your-views-and-the-results-that-count/

HM Government. 2012. Civil Service Reform Plan. https://www.official-documents.gov.uk or https://www.civilservice.gov.uk/reform.

HM Treasury. 2011. "Commitment to Action: Managing Taxpayers' Money Wisely." http://webarchive.nationalarchives.gov.uk/20130129110402/http://www.hm-treasury.gov.uk/psr_managing_taxpayers_money.htm.

———. 2013a. "Clear Line of Sight—the Alignment Project." http://webarchive.nationalarchives.gov.uk/20130129110402/http:/www.hm-treasury.gov.uk/psr_clear_line_of_sight_intro.htm.

———. 2013b. "Review of Financial Management in Government." https://www.gov.uk/government/uploads/system/uploads/attachment_data/file/266174/review_of_financial_management_in_government.pdf.

———. 2014. Treasury Minutes: Progress on Implementing Recommendations of Public Accounts Committee (July 2014). https://www.gov.uk/government/publications/treasury-minutes-progress-on-implementing-recommendations-of-public-accounts-committee-july-2014.

———. 2015a. Spending Review and Autumn Statement 2015. https://www.gov.uk/government/uploads/system/uploads/attachment_data/file/479749/52229_Blue_Book_PU1865_Web_Accessible.pdf.

———. 2015b. Civil Service Pay Guidance 2015 to 2016. https://www.gov.uk/government/publications/civil-service-pay-guidance-2015-to-2016/civil-service-pay-guidance-2015-to-2016.

Holmes, Lawrie. 2015. "An Ideal Catalyst." Financial Management. http://treasury.fm-magazine.com/?utm_source=TM&utm_medium=tweet&utm_camp.

House of Commons. 1968. Civil Service (Fulton Committee's Report). Deb June 26, 1968 vol. 767 cc454-65 Chairman Lord Fulton. http://hansard.millbanksystems.com/commons/1968/jun/26/civil-service-fulton-committees-report.

House of Lords. 1998. Select Committee on Public Service—Report Session 1997–98. http://www.publications.parliament.uk/pa/ld199798/ldselect/ldpubsrv/055/psrep01.htm.

Institute for Government. 2012. Study Shows Government Will Struggle to Make More Cuts without Radical New Thinking. Press release. November 2012. London: Institute for Government.

Manzoni, John. 2015. Forging Ahead with the Functions. Civil Service blog, April 16, 2015, https://civilservice.blog.gov.uk/2015/04/16/forging-ahead-with-the-functions/.

McCrea, Julian. 2016. "The Finance Function Forges Ahead." Blog January 28, 2016. http://www.instituteforgovernment.org.uk/blog/13137/the-finance-function-forges-ahead/.

NAO. 2009. *Comptroller and Auditor General Report: Commercial Skills for Complex Government Projects.* HC: 962, 2008–09, November 9, 2009. https://www.nao.org.uk/report/commercial-skills-for-complex-government-projects/.

———. 2012. *Comptroller and Auditor General Report: The Effectiveness of Internal Audit in Central Government* HC: 23, 2012–2013, June 20, 2012. https://www.nao.org.uk/report/the-effectiveness-of-internal-audit-in-central-government/.

———. 2013a. *Comptroller and Auditor General Report: Building Capability in the Senior Civil Service to Meet Today's Challenges.* HC: 129, 2013–14, June 19, 2013. https://www.nao.org.uk/report/building-capability-in-the-senior-civil-service-to-meet-to-days-challenges-2/.

———. 2013b. *Comptroller and Auditor General Report: Financial Management in Government.* HC: 131, Session 2013–14, June 13, 2013. https://www.nao.org.uk/report/financial-management-in-government-2/.

———. 2014a. *Comptroller and Auditor General Report: The Centre of Government,* NAO Session 2014–15, HC 171, June 2014. https://www.nao.org.uk/wp-content/uploads/2014/06/The-centre-of-government.pdf

———. 2014b. *Comptroller and Auditor General Report: Forecasting in Government to Achieve Value for Money.* HC: 969, Session 2013–2014 January 31, 2014. https://www.nao.org.uk/press-release/forecasting-government-achieve-value-money/.

———. 2014c. *Comptroller and Auditor General Report: Transforming Contract Management.* HC 268 Session 2014–15 September 4, 2014. https://www.nao.org.uk/wp-content/uploads/2014/09/Home-office-ministry-of-justice-transforming-contract-management.pdf.

———. 2015. *Comptroller and Auditor General Report: The Centre of Government: An Update.* NAO HC 1031 Session 2014–15, March 12, 2015. https://www.nao.org.uk/report/the-centre-of-government-an-update/.

Parliament. 2014. Public Accounts Committee—Fifty-Seventh Report: "The Ministry of Defence Equipment Plan 2013–23 and Major Projects Report 2013." http://www.publications.parliament.uk/pa/cm201314/cmselect/cmpubacc/1060/106002.htm.

Public Accounts Commission. 2014. "Value for Money Report 2014: Transformation." http://www.parliament.uk/documents/public-accounts-commission/TPAC14-VfMReport2014-Transformation.pdf.

Russell, Vivienne. 2016. "The Rising Role of FDs in Whitehall." *Public Finance,* January 26, 2016. http://www.publicfinance.co.uk/feature/2016/01/rising-role-fds-whitehall.

Saïd Business School. n.d. "Major Projects Leadership Academy." http://www.sbs.ox.ac.uk/programmes/execed/custom/clients-and-case-studies/major-projects-leadership-academy.

Stephen, Justine, Petr Bouchal, and David Bull. 2013. *Whitehall Monitor 2013, Annual Commentary and Analysis on the Size, Shape and Performance of Whitehall.* London: Institute for Government.

Swinford, Stephen. 2014. "MoD in £1.2 Billion Underspend as Thousands of Troops Are Sacked." May 13, 2014. *Daily Telegraph.* http://www.telegraph.co.uk/news/uknews/defence/10825822/MoD-in-1.2-billion-underspend-as-thousands-of-troops-are-sacked.html.

Thomas, Peter, and Jonathan Pearson. 2014. "Whitehall: Not the Final Cut." *Public Finance,* March 27, 2014. http://www.publicfinance.co.uk/2014/03/whitehall-not-final-cut.

ECO-AUDIT

Environmental Benefits Statement

The World Bank Group is committed to reducing its environmental footprint. In support of this commitment, the Publishing and Knowledge Division leverages electronic publishing options and print-on-demand technology, which is located in regional hubs worldwide. Together, these initiatives enable print runs to be lowered and shipping distances decreased, resulting in reduced paper consumption, chemical use, greenhouse gas emissions, and waste.

The Publishing and Knowledge Division follows the recommended standards for paper use set by the Green Press Initiative. The majority of our books are printed on Forest Stewardship Council (FSC)–certified paper, with nearly all containing 50–100 percent recycled content. The recycled fiber in our book paper is either unbleached or bleached using totally chlorine free (TCF), processed chlorine free (PCF), or enhanced elemental chlorine free (EECF) processes.

More information about the Bank's environmental philosophy can be found at http://crinfo.worldbank.org/wbcrinfo/node/4.

green press
INITIATIVE

* 9 7 8 1 4 6 4 8 0 8 0 4 3 *